The Wit & Wisdom of Ronald Reagan

★ ★ ★ ★ ★ ★ ★ ★ ★ ★ ★ ★ ★ ★ ★ ★

The Wit & Wisdom of Ronald Reagan

★ ★ ★ ★ ★ ★ ★ ★ ★ ★ ★ ★ ★ ★ ★ ★

JAMES C. HUMES

Since 1947
REGNERY
PUBLISHING, INC.

An Eagle Publishing Company • Washington, DC

Cataloging-in-Publication data on file with the Library of Congress

ISBN 978-1-59698-045-7

Published in the United States by
Regnery Publishing, Inc.
One Massachusetts Avenue, NW
Washington, DC 20001
www.regnery.com

Manufactured in the United States of America

10 9 8 7 6 5 4 3 2 1

Books are available in quantity for promotional or premium use. Write to Director of Special Sales, Regnery Publishing, Inc., One Massachusetts Avenue NW, Washington, DC 20001, for information on discounts and terms or call (202) 216-0600.

To Mary Stuart Humes Quillen, who as Managing Editor of the *Harvard Crimson*, in distinct contrast to those of other Ivy League universities, endorsed President Ronald Reagan for re-election in 1984.

I won a nickname, "The Great Communicator." But I never thought it was my style or the words I used that made a difference: it was the content. I wasn't a great communicator, but I communicated great things, and they didn't spring full bloom from my brow, they came from the heart of a great nation—from our experience, our wisdom, and our belief in the principles that have guided us for two centuries.

—Ronald Reagan's farewell address, January 11, 1989

Contents

Foreword by Michael Reagan x

Chapter 1: Reagan's Wisdom
Memorable and insightful Reagan quotations 1

Chapter 2: Reagan's Wit
His jokes, one-liners, and humorous turns of phrase 33

Chapter 3: Reagan's Saints and Sinners
*Reagan on the leading men and women
of his time and all time* 53

Chapter 4: Reagan's Friends and Foes
Reagan in the words of his contemporaries 69

Chapter 5: Reagan's Curiosities
Intrigues and trivia 87

Chapter 6: Reagan's Zingers
The stories behind his most memorable lines 119

Chapter 7: **Reagan's Yarns and Tales**
Entertaining stories by and about the man 133

Chapter 8: **Reagan's Speeches**
His greatest orations examined 177

Acknowledgments 209

Index 211

Foreword

My father has been likened by some to Abraham Lincoln and Franklin Roosevelt—Lincoln won the Civil War; Roosevelt, World War II; and Reagan the Cold War. All three were "liberators"—from slavery by Lincoln and from the tyranny of totalitarianism by Roosevelt and Reagan. That finding, however, is better left to the historians.

Yet as a son, I see some parallels between my father and Lincoln. Both were sons of Illinois and were raised in the small-town Midwestern values of self-reliance, self-discipline, and frugality. Such words were often heard by me as I asked for a bigger allowance. Other Beverly Hills actors' kids down the block, after all, were getting princely sums—umpteen times bigger than mine.

Often when I asked about allowance, I was treated to one of his anecdotes. If Dad never repeated a favorite story of his once aired nationally, we children enjoyed no such immunity. Dad used humor, like Lincoln, as an amiable armor. As soon as I saw that cocking of his head, followed by "Well, Michael, that reminds me . . . ," I knew I would get no further.

Dad's life would take him to Hollywood and the White House, but his tastes never left Dixon, Illinois. Just as he was plainspoken in his talk, he preferred the simple to the fancy in food and fashion. Meat and potatoes or macaroni and cheese was his idea of high cuisine, and in clothes, he left the designer labels to Nancy.

Like Lincoln too, Dad's principles were guided by his spiritual faith, even if he may have had his doubts about organized religion. Freedom did not come from government—it came from God, and those who suppressed freedom were "evil." Make no mistake about Dad—he was a committed Christian. He told me in 1988, "Michael, I love God and I love Jesus Christ."

There were some words that Dad used to quote from Abraham Lincoln. Lincoln wrote them just before he left Illinois for the last time. "I know there is a God. I know He hates injustice. I see a storm coming. If there is a place for me, I am ready."

Dad also believed that God had a plan for him. I was there in Kansas City in 1976, the only time Dad was ever defeated. That was for the Republican presidential nomination against Ford. God's timetable was better than Dad's. Had my father won the presidency in 1976, there's a good chance the Berlin Wall would not have come down and the Cold War would not have ended. Why? Because a number of key players like Pope John Paul and Margaret Thatcher were not yet in place. God did have a role for Dad to play.

Michael Reagan

© David Hume Kennerly/Getty Images

1
Reagan's Wisdom

★ ★ ★ ★ ★ ★ ★ ★ ★ ★ ★ ★ ★ ★ ★ ★ ★

Memorable and Insightful
Reagan Quotations

Not even his greatest admirers would characterize Ronald Reagan as an intellectual. The only presidents who might qualify as scholars and thinkers by the weight of their books and writings are John Adams, Thomas Jefferson, and James Madison in the early days of our republic and Theodore Roosevelt, Woodrow Wilson, and Richard Nixon in the past century.

Yet Reagan was more persuasive in shaping our political thinking than any of them. He was indeed the "Great Communicator." Reagan may not be described as a political philosopher, but his speeches moved American political thinking to the right.

Reagan, unlike so many of our recent presidents, was not a career politician. That was his advantage. He led a full life before entering politics at an age when most people contemplate retirement. He had been a sports broadcaster, actor, labor leader, and business spokesman. Those experiences added insights from different perspectives. When in his thirties, Reagan had been a Roosevelt Democrat. His experiences fighting the Communist influence in Hollywood eventually turned him into a conservative.

As a representative for General Electric and on the speech circuit, he addressed thousands of audiences across the country. He prepared these talks himself, and the following selections are the best of his observations and opinions. Generally, these reflections were shaped and honed by Reagan himself, not by speechwriters. Note the conversational ring and bite of these lines that would appeal to the ear as well as to the reading eye. Reagan, a speaker whose thousands of talks had polished his delivery, understood the rhetorical thrust of rhythm, repetition, and alliteration.

Abortion

Abortion is the taking of a human life.

Acting

An actor knows two important things—to be honest in what he's doing and to be in touch with the audience. That's not bad advice for a politician, either.

Affirmative Action

I am for affirmative action. I am against quotas. I have lived long enough to know a time in this country when quotas were used to discriminate, not end discrimination.

Age

Age has its privileges, not least among them the opportunity to distill whatever wisdom comes from a long life of experiences.

America

The United States is a natural athlete. No nation can claim all the advantages of America—population size, national resources, political stability, productive capacity, military strength, technological genius, and cultural influence.

⤙⤚

Freedom is the very essence of our nation. To be sure, ours is not a perfect nation. But even with our troubles, we remain the lesson of hope for oppressed people everywhere.

❦

God intended America to be free, to be the golden hope of mankind.

❦

I have long believed there was divine plan that placed this land here to be found by people of a special kind, that we have a rendezvous with destiny.

❦

Don't let anyone tell you that America's best days are behind her—that the American spirit has been vanquished. We've seen it triumph too often in our lives to stop believing in it now.

Americans

The task that has fallen to us Americans is to move the conscience of the world—to keep alive the hope and dream of freedom.

⟨≫⟩

Teddy Roosevelt once put it this way: "The American people are slow to wrath, but when their wrath is once kindled, it burns like a consuming flame."

⟨≫⟩

We're Americans, and we have a rendezvous with destiny.... No people who have ever lived on this earth have fought harder, paid a higher price for freedom, or done more to advance the dignity of man than Americans.

⟨≫⟩

Always remember that you are Americans, and it is your birthright to dream great dreams in this sweet and blessed land, truly the greatest, freest, strongest nation on earth.

Appeasement

A broader reading of history shows that appeasement, no matter how it is labeled, never fulfills the hopes of the appeasers.

Arms Treaties

Do arms agreements—even good ones—really bring or preserve peace? History would seem to say no.

Berlin Wall

It's as ugly as the idea behind it.

Big Government

The federal government has taken too much tax money from the people, too much authority from the states, and too much liberty with the Constitution.

❦

Are you entitled to the fruits of your own labor or does government have some presumptive right to spend and spend and spend?

Bigotry

I was raised from childhood by my parents who believed bigotry and prejudice were the worst things a person could be guilty of.

Capitalism

When was the last time you bought a car...or even a good cheese or video cassette recorder—and the label read "Made in the USSR"?

Citizenship

When those who are governed do too little, those who govern can—and often will—do too much.

Civil Liberties

Sometimes I can't help but feel the First Amendment is being turned on its head. Because ask yourselves: can it really be true that the First Amendment can permit Nazis and Ku Klux Klansmen to march on public property, advocate the extermination of people of the Jewish faith and the subjugation of blacks, while the same amendment forbids our children from saying a prayer in school?

Cold War

Here's my strategy on the Cold War: we win; they lose.

Communism

Many governments oppress their people and abuse human rights....But only one so-called revolution puts itself above God, insists on total control over the people's lives, and is driven by the desire to seize more and more lands....I have one question for those rulers: if Communism is the wave of the future, why do you still need walls to keep people in and armies of secret police to keep them quiet?

⟨❦⟩

The West will not contain Communism, it will transcend Communism. We will not bother to denounce it, we'll dismiss it as a sad, bizarre chapter in human history whose last pages are even now being written.

⟨❦⟩

Communists are not bound by our morality. They say that any crime—including lying—is moral if it advances the cause of socialism.

❧

The march of freedom and democracy will leave Marxism and Leninism on the ash heap of history.

Conservatism

You can't be for big government, big taxes, and big bureaucracy and still be for the little guy.

❧

You can't control the economy without controlling people.

Constitution

In this two-hundredth anniversary year [1987] of our Constitution, you and I stand on the shoulders of giants—men whose words and deeds put wind in the sails of freedom. . . . We will be guided tonight by their acts, and we will be guided forever by their words.

Courage

No arsenal, or no weapon in the arsenals of the world, is so formidable as the will and moral courage of free men and women.

Crime

It's time . . . that we acknowledge the solution to the crime problem will not be found in the social worker's files, the psychiatrist's notes, or the bureaucrat's budgets.

D-Day

You all knew that some things are worth dying for. One's country is worth dying for, and democracy is worth dying for, because it's the most deeply honorable form of government ever devised by man. All of you loved liberty. All of you were willing to fight tyranny, and you knew the people of your countries were behind you.

Decline

Nations crumble from within when the citizenry asks of government those things which the citizenry might better provide for itself.

Defense

Of the four wars in my lifetime, none came about because the United States was too strong.

Democracy

Optimism is in order because day by day democracy is proving itself to be a not at all fragile flower.

Democrats

Will Rogers once said he never met a man he didn't like. Well, if I could paraphrase Will, our friends in the other party have never met a tax they didn't like or hike.

Economics

The best sign that our economic program is working is that they don't call it "Reaganomics" anymore.

Facts

Specificity is the soul of credibility.

Faith

I can assure you that personal faith and conviction are strengthened, not weakened, in adversity.

⋘⋙

With faith as our guide, we can muster the wisdom and will to protect the deepest treasures of the human spirit—the freedom to build a better life in our time and the promise of life everlasting in His kingdom.

Family

All great change in America begins at the dinner table. So tomorrow night, in the kitchen, I hope the talking begins.

Fate

I do not believe in a fate that will fall on us no matter what we do. I do believe in a fate that will fall on us if we do nothing.

Foreign Policy

We cannot play innocents abroad in a world that's not innocent; nor can we be passive when freedom is under siege.

Freedom

History is on the side of the free because freedom is right and because freedom works.

⊷⊶

Progress is not foreordained. The key is freedom—freedom of thought, freedom of information, and freedom of communication.

Free Market

Individual freedom and the profit motive were the engines of progress which transformed an American wilderness into an economic dynamo that provided the American people with a standard of living that is still the envy of the world.

Future

History is a river that may take us as it will. But we have the power to navigate, to choose direction and make our passage together.

⌘

The future belongs to the free.

⌘

To those who are fainthearted and unsure, I have this message: if you're afraid of the future, then get out of the way, stand aside. The people of this country are ready to move again.

⌘

You can play a special part in this future. You'll be its author: take full advantage of the wonderful life that lies in store for you.

God

We have to keep in mind we are a nation under God, and if we ever forget that we'll be just a nation under.

Heroes

Heroes may not be braver than anyone else, they're just braver five minutes longer.

Himself

I was a near hopeless hemophilic liberal.

Hollywood

[T]hose pictures with no four-letter words, no nude scenes, no blatant sex, no vulgarity, were better theater than today's realism.

Husband

It does take quite a man to remain attractive and to be loved by a woman who has heard him snore, seen him unshaven, tended him while he was sick, and washed his dirty underwear.

Marijuana

If adults want to take such chances, that is their business.

National Anthem

I don't know all the national anthems in the world, but I don't know of any that end with a question. . . . Could we see that banner through the smoke and the bomb burst when morning came? . . . We know it's still flying, but it's up to us to see that it continues to fly over a land that is free and brave.

New Deal

The press is trying to paint me as now trying to undo the New Deal. I remind them I voted for FDR four times. I'm trying to undo the "Great Society."

Panama Canal

We should end those negotiations and tell the general: we bought it, we paid for it, we built it, and we intend to keep it.

Poverty

We have to realize that this country in its private sector has been fighting the most successful war on poverty the world has seen for the last two hundred years.

Pragmatism

I'd rather get 80 percent of what I want than to go over the cliff with my flag flying.

Prayer

The Supreme Court opens its proceedings with a religious invocation—Hear ye, hear ye, hear ye. God bless this honorable court and save these United States.

And the members of Congress open their sessions with a prayer. We have a prayer every time this door opens. I just happen to believe the schoolchildren of the United States are entitled to the same privileges as Supreme Court justices and congressmen.

⤎⋙◈⋘⤏

The Constitution was never meant to prevent people from praying; its declared purpose was to protect their freedom to pray.

Presidency

You surround yourself with the best people you can find, delegate authority, and don't interfere.

⁓⊰⧉⊱⁓

At my age, I didn't go to Washington to play politics as usual.

⁓⊰⧉⊱⁓

Franklin Delano Roosevelt...John Kennedy, that bright spirit, and Teddy Roosevelt, and Harry Truman: they all loved the presidency, loved the bully pulpit of the office, loved looking out for the interests of our country. So do I.

Religious Oppression

You may bully their rabbis and dissidents. You may forbid the name of Jesus to pass their lips. But you will never destroy the love of God and freedom that burns in their hearts. They will triumph over you.

Smoking

Yes, I know many adults continue to smoke, but I don't know any who don't wish they could quit [letter to his daughter Patti].

Soviet Union

An evil empire.

⧉

I think one line recently written by former President Nixon was very true. He said of our country, we want peace; he said the Soviet Union *needs* peace. And they do, with this great, massive buildup, the greatest the world has ever seen in military might.

Special Interests

When I took the oath of office, I pledged loyalty to only one special interest group: "we the people."

Statesmanship

The challenge of statesmanship is to have the vision to dream of a better, safer world and the courage, persistence, and patience to turn that dream into reality.

Taxes

Common sense told us that when you put a big tax on something, the people will produce less of it. So, we cut the people's tax rates, and the people produced more than ever before.

Terrorism

Terrorism is the preferred weapon of weak and evil men.

Trade

We too often talk about trade while using the vocabulary of war. In war, for one side to win, the other must lose. But commerce is not warfare. Trade is an economic alliance that benefits both countries; there are no losers, only winners. And trade helps strengthen the free world.

Tyranny

And to every person trapped in tyranny...we send our love and support and tell them they are not alone. Our message must be: your struggle is our struggle, your dream is our dream, and someday, you, too, will be free. As Pope John Paul told his beloved Poles, we are blessed by divine heritage. We are children of God and we cannot be slaves.

❦

Regimes planted by bayonets do not take root.

Welfare State

I'm sure everyone feels sorry for the individual who has fallen by the way-side or who can't keep up in our competitive society, but my own compassion goes beyond that to the millions of unsung men and women who get up every morning, send the kids to school, go to work, try and keep up the payments on their house, pay exorbitant taxes to make possible compassion for the less fortunate, and as a result have to sacrifice many of their own desires and dreams and hopes. Government owes them something better than always finding a new way to make them share the fruit of their toils with others.

$\cdot$

I think the best possible social program is a job.

$\cdot$

America is more than just government on the one hand and helpless individuals on the other.

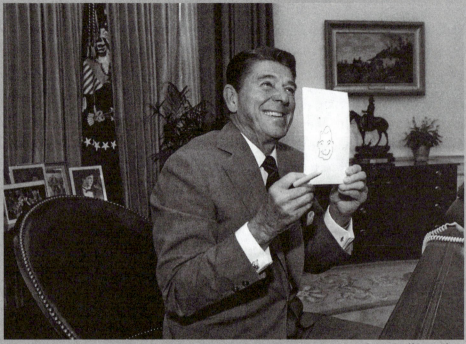

Courtesy Ronald Reagan Library

2

Reagan's Wit

★ ★ ★ ★ ★ ★ ★ ★ ★ ★ ★ ★ ★ ★ ★

*His jokes, one-liners, and
humorous turns of phrase*

No president in our history has coined more epigrammatic lines that poked fun at big government, bureaucracy, and the tyranny of taxation. Presidents from Harry Truman to Richard Nixon all waged rhetorical attack against Communism, but only Ronald Reagan wielded wit as a weapon to bring down the Iron Curtain.

Ronald Reagan was the first person from the entertainment world to be elected president. Unlike so many politicians who regularly pontificate, Reagan knew a speaker had to capture and keep the attention of the audience. He was never a bore behind a microphone.

Few of the humorous sallies that follow originated from speechwriters; Reagan himself honed and polished them on the speech circuit. He was America's top convention draw and after-dinner speaker before he ever ran for governor. With that patented cock of his head and a pause followed by "Well . . ." combined with his actor's sense of timing, no president ever mastered better the art of the one-liner.

Age

I heard one presidential candidate [Gary Hart in 1987] say what this country needed was a president for the nineties. I was set to run again. I thought he said a president *in* his nineties.

❧

Last year, you all helped me begin celebrating the thirty-first anniversary of my thirty-ninth birthday. [Laughter] And I must say that all of those pile up, an increase of numbers, don't bother me at all, because I recall that Moses was eighty when God commissioned him for public service, and he lived to be 120.

❧

"Ron," my caller said, "How come you look younger every day when I see a new picture of you riding on horseback?" I said, Jimmy, that's easy. I just keep riding older horses.

⚬✵⚬

Larry [Speakes, Reagan's press secretary] also said that preparing me for a press conference was like reinventing the wheel. It's not true. I was around when the wheel was invented, and it was easier.

⚬✵⚬

And I also remember something that Thomas Jefferson once said. He said, "We should never judge a president by his age, only by his works." And ever since he told me that, I've stopped worrying.

Atheism

Sometimes when I'm faced with an unbeliever, an atheist, I am tempted to invite him to the greatest gourmet dinner that one could ever serve, and when we finished eating that magnificent dinner, to ask him if he believes there's a cook.

Budget

Balancing the budget is like protecting your virtue. You just have to learn to say no.

Bureaucracy

I've always thought that the common sense and wisdom of government were summed up in a sign they used to have hanging on that gigantic Hoover Dam. It said, "Government Property. Do Not Remove."

California

The symbol on our state flag is the Golden Bear. It is not a cow to be milked.

Congress

I have wondered at times what the Ten Commandments would have looked like if Moses had run them through the U.S. Congress.

Constitution

You know, Senator [Ted] Kennedy was at a dinner recently—the ninetieth birthday party for former governor and ambassador Averell Harriman. Teddy Kennedy said Averell's age was only half as old as Ronald Reagan's ideas. And you know, he's absolutely right. The Constitution is almost two hundred years old, and that's where I get my ideas.

Deficits

At home our enemy is no longer Redcoats but Red Ink.

Depression

A recession is when your neighbor loses his job. A depression is when you lose yours.

Doctorate (Honorary)

After all the time I spent with G. W. doctors, it seems fitting that I now become one [at George Washington University].

Economist

An economist is a person with a Phi Beta Kappa key on one end of his watch chain and no watch on the other.

Education

If you serve a child a rotten hamburger in America, federal, state, and local agencies will investigate you, summon you, close you down, whatever. But if you provide a child with a rotten education, nothing happens, except that you're liable to be given more money to do it with.

Football

I couldn't play baseball because I couldn't see good enough. That's why I turned to football. The ball was bigger and so were the fellows.

Foreign Policy

There's been some criticism, however, that we don't have a definite foreign policy—that we haven't been doing enough about that—and that's not true at all. Just the other day, before he left for China, Al Haig sent a message to Brezhnev that said, "Roses are red, violets are blue, stay out of El Salvador and Poland, too."

Freedom

Having a little bit of freedom is like being a little bit pregnant.

Government

If it moves, tax it. If it keeps moving, regulate it. If it stops moving, subsidize it.

❦

It's like a baby—it's an alimentary canal with an appetite on one end and no sense of responsibility at the other.

❦

Government does not solve problems—it subsidizes them.

Governor

I don't know. I've never played governor [when asked in January 1967 what his first priority as governor was].

Great Society

The Great Society is great only in power, in size, and in cost.

Health

Since I came to the White House, I got two hearing aids, a colon operation, skin cancer, a prostate operation, and I was shot; and the damned thing is I've never felt better in my life.

Hearing

It's no secret that I wear a hearing aid. Well, just the other day, all of the sudden, it went haywire. We discovered the KGB had put a listening device in my listening device.

Himself

I've laid down the law, though, to everyone. From now on, about anything that happens, no matter what time it is, wake me, even if it's in the middle of a cabinet meeting.

History

History is no easy subject. Even in my day it wasn't, and we had so much less of it to learn then.

Law and Order

Today's hard-liner on law and order is yesterday's liberal who was mugged last night.

Liberalism

The trouble with our liberal friends is not that they're ignorant, it's just that they know so much that isn't so.

Looks

Tip O'Neill once asked me how I keep myself looking so young for the cameras. I told him I have a good makeup team. It's the same people who've been repairing the Statue of Liberty.

Middle Age

Middle age is when you're faced with two temptations and you choose the one that will get you home at 9:30.

National Debt

When I was in fifth grade, I'm not sure that I knew what a national debt was. Of course, when I was in fifth grade, we didn't have one.

Poise

I have learned that one of the most important rules in politics is poise—which means looking like an owl after you have behaved like a jackass.

Politics

Politics is supposed to be the second oldest profession in the world. I have come to realize that it bears a very close resemblance to the first.

❧

Politics is not a bad profession. If you succeed, there are many rewards. If you disgrace yourself, you can always write a book.

Poverty

Some years ago, the federal government declared war on poverty, and poverty won.

Presidency

When I leave the White House, they will put on my chair in the Cabinet Room "Ronald Reagan slept here."

School

I confess, I was not as attentive as I might have been during my classroom days. I seem to remember my parents being told, "Young Ron is trying—very trying."

Soviet Union

The Soviet Union would remain a one-party nation even if an opposition party were permitted, because everyone would join the opposition party.

Status Quo

Status quo, you know, is Latin for "the mess we're in."

Taxation

England may be the mother of parliaments, but from the Boston Tea Party to this administration, it's the United States that's been the mother of tax revolts.

⊱⊰

They have a kind of layaway plan for your lives, which never changes. It's called "Americans make; government takes."

⊱⊰

I feel like we just played the World Series of tax reform—and the American people won [1986].

Taxpayer

The taxpayer: that's someone who works for the government but doesn't have to take the civil service exam.

Washington, D.C.

I've learned in Washington that that's the only place where sound travels faster than light.

❧

I should warn you that things in this city aren't often the way they seem. Where but in Washington would they call the department that's in charge of everything outdoors the Department of the *Interior*?

Welfare State

We don't celebrate "dependence day" on the Fourth of July—we celebrate Independence Day!

Work

It's true hard work never killed anybody, but I figure why take the chance?

Courtesy Ronald Reagan Library

3

Reagan's Saints and Sinners

★ ★ ★ ★ ★ ★ ★ ★ ★ ★ ★ ★ ★ ★ ★ ★ ★ ★

*Reagan on the leading men
and women of his time and all time*

Few politicians—with the exception of those presidents who might grace our currency with their portraits—made it into Ronald Reagan's pantheon of heroes. One exception is Margaret Thatcher. Political foes like Jimmy Carter, Walter Mondale, and Michael Dukakis invited snappy putdowns, yet some of his adversaries, such as Speaker Tip O'Neill, drew words of affectionate appreciation.

Reagan preferred the world of Hollywood to that of Washington, and it is no surprise that some of his favorite personalities were from the entertainment world, like Frank Sinatra and Robert Taylor. He admired John Wayne and Jimmy Stewart because they portrayed so well the courage, resolve, and daring he saw inherent in all Americans. Reagan's real heroes, however, were those without famous names, the fireman who rescues children from a burning house, the cleaning woman who sends her son to college, or the Ranger who climbed Pointe du Hoc in Normandy.

George H. W. Bush

The finest vice president this country has ever had [during the 1988 presidential campaign].

Dr. Martin Luther King Jr.

Where others—white and black—preached hatred, he taught the principles of love and nonviolence.

Franklin D. Roosevelt

During the fireside chats, his strong, gentle, confident voice resonated across the nation with an eloquence that brought comfort and resilience to a nation caught up in a storm and reassured us that we could lick any problem.

Jimmy Carter

PRESIDENT AND REAGAN'S OPPONENT IN 1980

A recession is when your neighbor loses his job. A depression is when you lose yours. Recovery is when Jimmy Carter loses his job.

∽∾✠∾∽

In place of competence, he has given us ineptitude. Instead of steadiness, he has offered vacillation. When America looks for confidence, he gives us fear.

Richard Nixon

When Richard Nixon went there [China] and made the opening, I immediately supported him in that and publicly went to bat for the value in doing what he was doing.

Sir Winston Churchill

PRIME MINISTER OF GREAT BRITAIN

History recalls his greatness in ways no dictator will ever know. And he left us a message of hope for the future

His Fulton speech was a fire bell in the night, a Paul Revere warning that tyranny was once again on the march.

Mac Baldrige

SECRETARY OF COMMERCE UNDER REAGAN

Honesty, courage, industry, and humility—these were his yardsticks. And if you had these simple qualities, you'd made it in his eyes, whether you were rich or poor, famous or unknown.

Michael Dukakis

DEMOCRATIC PRESIDENTIAL CANDIDATE IN 1988

I'm afraid that Dukakis's foreign policy views are a little too far left for me. He wants no U.S. military presence in Korea anymore, no U.S. military presence in Central America, and no U.S. military presence at the Pentagon.

Barry Goldwater

REPUBLICAN SENATOR FROM ARIZONA

In 1964 came a voice in the wilderness—Barry Goldwater; the great Barry Goldwater, the first major party candidate of our time who was a true-blue, undiluted conservative. He spoke from principle, and he offered vision.

Daniel "Chappie" James

AFRICAN AMERICAN AIR FORCE GENERAL

He became a four-star general, joining that exclusive club that includes Ulysses S. Grant and John J. Pershing. He had known times when he was not allowed to enter an officers' club. That didn't make him bitter. He was able to see past that to the real greatness of this land.

Jesus Christ

A young man whose father is a carpenter grows up working in his father's shop. He has no formal education. He owns no property of any kind. One day he puts down his tools and walks out of his father's shop. He starts preaching on street corners and in the countryside. . . . This uneducated, propertyless young man who preached on street corners . . . had a greater effect on the entire world than all the rulers, kings, and emperors, all the conquerors, the generals and admirals, all the scholars, scientists, and philosophers who ever lived—all put together.

John F. Kennedy

Underneath the tousled boyish haircut, it is still old Karl Marx [in a letter to Richard Nixon in 1960].

❦

Many men are great, but few capture the imagination and the spirit of the times.... History is not only made by people, it *is* people. And so history is, as a young John Kennedy demonstrated, as heroic as you want it to be, as heroic as you are.

Lowell Weicker

DEMOCRATIC SENATOR FROM CONNECTICUT

He's a pompous, no-good fathead.

Jimmy Stewart

ACTOR

Jimmy Stewart's modesty meant he never really understood the greatness that others saw in him.

Henry Kissinger

SECRETARY OF STATE

He has an amazing knowledge of all the players.

Walter "Fritz" Mondale

VICE PRESIDENT UNDER CARTER AND REAGAN'S OPPONENT IN 1984

Here is a man who all his years in the Senate voted against every weapons system, except the slingshot.

Sam Nunn

DEMOCRATIC SENATOR FROM GEORGIA

Highly overrated.

Thomas "Tip" O'Neill

DEMOCRATIC SPEAKER OF THE HOUSE

Tip, if I had a ticket to heaven and you didn't have one too, I would give mine away and go to hell with you.

Muammar Qadhafi

PRESIDENT OF LIBYA

Mad dog of the Middle East.

Donald Regan

SECRETARY OF THE TREASURY AND CHIEF OF STAFF UNDER REAGAN

I was a little disappointed in that movie *The Last Emperor*. I thought it was going to be about Don Regan.

Nancy Reagan

Life would be miserable if there wasn't a Nancy's birthday! What if she had never been born? I don't want to think about it.

Nell Wilson Reagan

REAGAN'S MOTHER

She was my inspiration and provided me with a very real and deep faith.

Robert Taylor

ACTOR

He was a man who respected his profession and was a master of it.

Theodore Roosevelt

Most people remember him as a man of strength and vitality, and yes, some have an image of a warlike man always spoiling for a fight. Well, let us remember he won the Nobel Peace Prize, an honor bestowed upon him for his courageous and energetic efforts to end the Russo-Japanese war. He knew the relationship between peace and strength.

Caspar W. Weinberger

SECRETARY OF DEFENSE UNDER REAGAN

My personal Disraeli.

Anwar Sadat

PRESIDENT OF EGYPT

In a world filled with hatred, he was a man of hope. In a world trapped in the animosities of the past, he was a man of foresight, a man who sought to improve a world tormented by malice and pettiness.

Richard Viguerie

CONSERVATIVE ACTIVIST

He tried to write in sorrow, not in anger about my betrayal of the conservative cause. He used crocodile tears for ink.

Margaret Thatcher

PRIME MINISTER OF GREAT BRITAIN

She's the other woman in my life.

Mother Teresa

Most of us talk about kindness and compassion, but Mother Teresa, the saint of the gutters, lives it.

George Washington

We come filled with pride and gratitude to honor George Washington, father of our country, knowing that because of what he did we're free and we're Americans.

❦

He did more than live up to the standards of the time; he set them.

❦

The image of George Washington kneeling in prayer in the snow is one of the most famous in American history.

❦

Yes, he is first in our hearts and will be first for all time. But as Abraham Lincoln said, "To add brightness to the sun, or glory to the name of Washington, is . . . impossible. Let none attempt it . . . pronounce the name, and . . . leave it shining on."

Courtesy Ronald Reagan Library

4

Reagan's Friends and Foes

★ ★ ★ ★ ★ ★ ★ ★ ★ ★ ★ ★ ★ ★ ★ ★ ★ ★ ★

Reagan in the words of his contemporaries

Ronald Reagan had no shortage of enemies, but he had more friends. He had friends not only in both parties, but also on both coasts—from ambassadors and senators to actors and directors.

Some of his colleagues in the Hollywood community, like Bob Cummings and Olivia de Havilland, sensed early on his capacity for leadership. For those in the conservative movement, Reagan would succeed Barry Goldwater as their champion and hero. But Reagan's appeal would far transcend the ideological Right. He made average Americans proud of their country. He rhapsodized on the heroic in their lives. History will render its final judgment, but it would be hard not to appreciate Reagan's impact on defeating the Communists in the Cold War.

He is the kindest and most impersonal man I ever met.

James A. Baker
Reagan's chief of staff and secretary of the treasury

A man whose simple tastes are said by his enemies to match his intellect. That judgment has cost them many a victory.

Michael Deaver
Deputy chief of staff under Reagan

Reagan is only an actor who memorizes speeches written by other people, just like he memorized the lines that were fed to him by his screenwriters in the movies. Sure, he makes a good speech, but who's writing his speeches?

Edmund "Pat" Brown
Governor of California and Reagan's opponent in 1966

The best speechwriter who ever worked in the White House—at least since Lincoln—was Ronald Reagan himself.

James A. Baker
Reagan's chief of staff and secretary of the treasury

A prophet in his time. . . . He's a man whose life embodies freedom, who nurtured freedom as few presidents ever have.

George H. W. Bush

I regard Reagan as a puzzle. I am still trying to understand the man.

Lou Cannon
California journalist and Reagan biographer

I never knew who he was, I could never get through to him.

Patti Davis
Reagan's daughter

When you meet the president you ask yourself, "How did it ever occur to anyone that he should be governor, much less president?"

Henry Kissinger
Secretary of state under Nixon and Ford

An amiable dunce.

Clark Clifford
Secretary of defense under Lyndon Johnson

He truly believes in the best of everybody he meets, which is a wonderful way to live—if a trifle unrealistic.

Michael Deaver
Deputy chief of staff under Reagan

Sunshine and clear sky. We shook hands like friends. He said something, I don't know what. But at once I felt him to be a very authentic human being.

Mikhail Gorbachev

The Reagan speechwriter's major function is to plagiarize the president's old speeches and give them back to him to say.

Tony Dolan
Reagan speechwriter

Ronnie doesn't dye his hair. He's just prematurely orange.

Gerald Ford

In the Cold War, Reagan turned out to be our Churchill.

Dinesh D'Souza
Economist and political scientist

Often I'd go to him and I would expect serious answers to questions, which I would get from Nixon and Ford, but he would seem disinterested and would toss off some anecdote from his Hollywood days.

General Alexander Haig Jr.
Secretary of state under Reagan

Ronald Reagan was much more interested in the big picture than the details—a big idea man who left the fine points to others.

James A. Baker
Reagan's chief of staff and secretary of the treasury

Reagan himself was a highly organized and disciplined person underneath his relaxed and genial manner.

Edwin Meese
White House counsel and attorney general under Reagan

[Reagan was] a one-man battalion against [Communists in Hollywood]. He was very vocal and very clear-thinking on it.

Sterling Hayden
Actor

He had an extremely moderate lifestyle. He paced himself in a very disciplined way. He was incredibly organized. I have never seen a man so totally focused.

Martin Anderson
Domestic advisor under Reagan

He doesn't treat himself like a statue of himself.

Jeane Kirkpatrick
UN ambassador under Reagan

I'm running against an actor, and you know who shot Lincoln, don't you?

Edmund "Pat" Brown
Governor of California and Reagan's opponent in 1966

It would be foolish to deny that his success was fundamentally rooted in a command of public ideas. . . . Whether we agreed with him or not, Ronald Reagan was a successful candidate and an effective president above all else because he stood for a set of ideas. He stated them in 1980—and it turned out that he meant them—and he wrote most of them not only into public law but into the national consciousness.

Edward Kennedy
Democratic senator from Massachusetts

A master magician.

Anthony Lewis
New York Times columnist

He knows so little and accomplishes so much.

Robert MacFarlane
National security advisor under Reagan

What bothered me about Reagan was his lack of curiosity about what we [he and the other authors present] did and what we thought about the world. There was a kind of impenetrable curtain between us and the president [after a White House dinner for American authors].

Robert Massie
Historian of Russia

He was to popular politics what Henry James was to American literature. He is the master. No one could do what he did, move people that way, talk to them so that they understood.

Peggy Noonan
Reagan speechwriter

Beneath the surface you find someone who isn't stupid, who has great good sense and profoundly good intentions. What he does not perceive with his intelligence, he feels by nature.

François Mitterrand
President of France

I shared an image of him as a pitchman who was a good communicator, who was more interested in selling himself and his administration than he was in accomplishment.

Bob Moretti
Democratic Speaker of the House in California

Ronald Reagan won the Cold War without firing a shot.

Margaret Thatcher

The Teflon president.

Pat Schroeder
Democratic congresswoman from Colorado

Ronald Reagan was Herbert Hoover with a smile.

Thomas "Tip" O'Neill
Democratic Speaker of the House

Ronald Reagan is an ignoramus, a conscious and persistent falsifier of fact, a deceiver of the electorate, and, one suspects of himself.

John Osborne
New Republic writer

He looks like a fat little Dutchman [the origin of his boyhood nickname].

Jack Reagan
Reagan's father

When I opened that door for our first date, I knew he was the man I wanted to marry.

Nancy Davis Reagan

Reagan was a friendly man with one close friend. He married her.

George Will
Columnist and former Reagan speechwriter

He was a compulsive entertainer.

Peggy Noonan
Reagan speechwriter

Ronald Reagan for governor? No. Jimmy Stewart for governor! Ronald Reagan for best friend.

Jack Warner
Movie producer

I predict historians are going to be totally baffled by how the American people fell in love with this man and followed him the way we did.

Lesley Stahl
CBS news anchor

In him greatness and simplicity are one.

Mother Teresa

It is humiliating to think of this unlettered, self-assured bumpkin being our president.

Nicholas von Hoffman
Washington Post columnist

The stricken fields of American politics are littered with the bleached bones of those who underestimated Ronald Reagan.

George Will
Columnist and former Reagan speechwriter

Courtesy Ronald Reagan Library

5

Reagan's Curiosities

★ ★ ★ ★ ★ ★ ★ ★ ★ ★ ★ ★ ★ ★ ★

Intrigues and trivia

The world knows every president's great triumphs and failures, but the obscure personal tidbits, weird coincidences, or small peculiarities don't quite make it to the cover of *People* magazine in the way most celebrities' personal details do. With Reagan, it was different. Reagan's life was material for gossip columns long before he entered the political arena. Sportscasters' and movie actors' lives interest most readers in the way politicians' lives do not. The trivia of Ronald Reagan's life is as rich as his resume.

Alzheimer's Month

In October 1988, President Reagan declared November Alzheimer's month. Six years later, in November 1994, he disclosed that he had developed the disease.

Blindsided

It is not generally known how bad Reagan's eyes were. He was turned down for service abroad by the Army for his poor eyesight and instead did training films in California. In Hollywood, his myopia was a handicap early in his career. The thick contact lenses of the late 1930s caused Reagan eye pain and headaches. He wore them only for short periods when he had to identify people at a distance. Most of the time, off-set crew members would wave their hands to direct him to one side or the other.

Brawny, Not Scrawny

Football fan Ronald Reagan had read the biography of Notre Dame football coach Knute Rockne and was convinced it would make a great movie. He envisioned Pat O'Brien playing the lead role and went to Warner Brothers to sell them on it. They bought the rights and liked the idea of O'Brien as Rockne.

But they didn't see Reagan playing the role of George Gipp, the famous Fighting Irish halfback who died in the middle of the season.

"Ron," they said, "you're a bit too scrawny to play the big halfback." Reagan worked out, showed them photos of his college days playing halfback, and then posed for them in shoulder pads and helmet. He got the role of George Gipp in the 1940 film *Knute Rockne: All American* and forever bore the nickname "the Gipper."

The Chimp and the Chump?

Reagan co-starred with many of the biggest Hollywood stars, including Errol Flynn, Olivia de Havilland, Robert Cummings, Lee Marvin, Barbara Stanwyck, Doris Day, Humphrey Bogart, and Bette Davis—to list a few.

But, as his detractors liked to point out, he was the first actor whose co-star was a chimp. In the comedy *Bedtime for Bonzo*, Reagan played a professor who tries to prove that environment is a more powerful influence than heredity. His tests involve a chimpanzee named Bonzo. Liberal critics said that Reagan was out-performed by the chimp.

Co-Billing

In American history, the connection between the presidents and the wives they chose often provides curious interest. Franklin Roosevelt married a distant cousin of the same name who was a niece of Theodore Roosevelt. Andrew Johnson wed a woman who had taught him to read and write. Grover Cleveland married the much younger ward of his law partner.

But Reagan was the only one to marry a woman who had co-starred with him in a film. In the 1957 movie *Hellcats of the Navy*, actress Nancy Davis was the leading lady and love interest of Reagan's naval aviator. The couple had already dated off-screen, and they were married afterward.

Co-Respondent Johnny

Reagan's first wife, Jane Wyman, won an Oscar for her performance as a deaf-mute farm girl in the 1948 film *Johnny Belinda*. Her subsequent fame and success led to estrangement in their marriage. As Reagan spent more time as the Screen Actors Guild leader, working to keep out Communist influence, his wife's movie career blossomed.

Reagan was devastated by Jane's desire for a divorce, commenting, "I think I should name *Johnny Belinda* as the co-respondent."

Death's Icy Fingers

Just about the whole world knows how Reagan almost lost his life in an assassination attempt in March 1981. Yet few are aware of his first brush with death.

In 1947, Reagan agreed to do a role and script he didn't like in a B movie, *That Hagen Girl*, with a grown-up Shirley Temple.

While filming one particularly strenuous scene, Reagan was asked to rescue Temple from a lake. The director made Reagan dive seven times into the icy water until he was convinced the scene was just right. The always amenable Reagan plunged into the lake as directed, and the next day he woke up with a high fever. He had contracted a virulent strain of viral pneumonia, and he barely survived.

Director's Dream

In his fifty-three feature films, Reagan never arrived late, never arrived hungover, and never was a problem. Directors called him "One-Shot Ronnie" because he was always prepared; his lines were always memorized when it was time to shoot a scene.

Divorced Man as President

Ronald Reagan was the oldest person ever elected president. He was also the first actor ever to win the White House. Another first in presidential history: he was the first divorced man to be commander in chief.

His first wife, actress Jane Wyman, sued for divorce in 1949. She was the mother of two of his children, Maureen and their adopted son Michael. In the Reagan Library and Memorial near Santa Barbara, the name Jane Wyman is found only once.

Dixon Duo

It did not hurt Reagan's movie career that the movie industry's most celebrated gossip columnist, Luella Parsons, also hailed from the small town of Dixon, Illinois. She was a powerful force in Hollywood: words of praise from Luella (or her hated rival Hedda Hopper) could point a producer or agent to a rising star. She touted the nuptials of Ronnie Reagan and Jane Wyman as "the perfect marriage" and did everything she could to polish both Ronnie's and Jane's stardom. She was devastated by their eventual divorce.

Dutch Dismissed

It is a little known fact that the "Great Communicator" was fired from his first job for not communicating well. "Dutch" Reagan was gaining some popularity with the listening audience of his Des Moines morning radio talk show. In the conversational, unscripted part of the show, his relaxed baritone worked well. The problem was the advertisements; the sponsors found his delivery stiff and unconvincing. Reagan knew they were right. He later found that by looking down at the advertisements and then looking up from them and "conversationalizing" a line or two he had just read, he could simulate a style that suggested he wasn't just reading them.

Empty Church

The little brown church in Los Angeles County had only about five attendants—including the preacher—when Ronald Reagan married Nancy Davis in March 1952 (he had proposed two months before). They included the bride, groom, best man William Holden, and Holden's wife, who was the matron of honor.

The Eyes Have It

Before delivering a major address, if Reagan would be reading from a prepared speech, he would put in two different contact lenses—one nearsighted for the right eye and one farsighted for the left eye.

With his right eye he would look down at the script, and with the left he would look out at the audience members to size up their reaction.

The First President

President Reagan got to know several presidents, but the first president he ever met was not an American. While he was in Britain filming *The Hasty Heart*, he took a trip to Ireland, where he was introduced to Éamon de Valera, who had been the first president of the Irish Republic.

Flavor of the Day

Just about everybody knows that Reagan kept a bowl of jelly beans on his desk in the Oval Office, but few are aware that he was responsible for a new flavor of jelly bean. Blueberries were the president's favorite fruit. He liked everything blueberry: pancakes, muffins, or just berries in a bowl. Accordingly, jelly bean manufacturer Jelly Belly created a blueberry jelly bean in time for Easter 1986.

Flight of Inspiration

In one of his most lyrical addresses, Reagan ended with a line of verse from the poem "High Flight," written by World War II pilot John Gillespie Magee Jr. The first and last lines read, "Oh! I have slipped the surly bonds of earth/ Put out my hand, and touched the face of God."

Magee was shot down in 1941. The poem was received by his father, the rector of St. John's Episcopal Church across from the White House, who was a friend of President Roosevelt's.

Reagan first heard the poem in 1945, recited from memory by actor and airman Tyrone Power at a welcoming party thrown by Gary and Rocky Cooper upon Power's return from war. Reagan was at the party and was moved by Magee's poem. Forty-five years later, after the explosion of the space shuttle *Challenger*, Reagan reminded America of that bit of poetry.

Hi Ho, Silver!

Of all the horses Reagan ever owned, his favorite was El Alamein. This white stallion had been a gift from President Portillo of Mexico in 1980. When Reagan approached his stable to ride him, El Alamein would rear up and walk on his hind legs to greet him. Reagan had a special rinse with the trade name Quicksilver, which he rubbed into El Alamein's coat. After five minutes, the blue rinse dried and the horse glowed a satiny silver.

"Killer" at the Box Office

Reagan's last movie, *The Killers*, was a lemon. The casting director talked him into playing the villain, insisting that it would be a challenge for him to play against character. The movie (also starring John Cassavetes and Lee Marvin) flopped. Said Reagan later, "I think the viewers kept waiting for me to repent and become a good guy in the end."

The Late Show

Departing from California precedent, Reagan decided to move up his swearing in from noon to just past midnight on January 2, 1967. The reason Reagan gave was that he wanted to prevent outgoing Pat Brown from burdening him with any last-minute appointments. Actually, Brown could have done that in the two months following his defeat in November. Some attributed the time change to the possible involvement of Jeanne Dixon, Mrs. Reagan's favorite astrologer.

So at 12:02 AM, Reagan took the oath. Right afterward, he said to his former fellow actor and friend George Murphy, who was sitting in the front row, "Well, George, here we are on the *Late Show* again."

Mr. Presidents

One of the most bizarre events in national political convention history was the drama in Detroit in 1980 of a future president considering a past president as his running mate for vice president.

Former governor Ronald Reagan had his nomination locked up long before Republican delegates began assembling in Detroit. The only question mark would be his choice for running mate. George H. W. Bush, who had been Reagan's chief opponent for the nomination, had continued in the race most of the year. Now Bush's people were maneuvering behind the scenes to secure the number-two spot for him. In his favor were polls showing that Bush would add a couple of percentage points to Reagan's numbers, particularly in the East. The problem was Reagan himself. Reagan preferred someone like Senator Paul Laxalt of Nevada, with whom he clicked. The two had gotten to know each other while serving as governors. Laxalt, however, did nothing politically for Reagan.

At the convention, former president Gerald Ford delivered a robust speech that promised an all-out effort to beat President Carter, whom Ford despised. In an earlier meeting with the former president, Reagan found himself drawn to the man he had opposed four years earlier for the nomination. Both came from similar small-town Midwestern backgrounds.

Reagan sent some feelers toward Ford, who did not completely remove himself from the swirling newspaper speculation that followed. One enthusiast was Ford's former secretary of state, Henry Kissinger, who began mapping out some divisions of duty, particularly in foreign policy. Politically, of course, it was a sure winner, but practically, it was a non-starter. Somewhat reluctantly, Reagan settled for Bush.

No Plain Jane

Reagan's first romantic comedy ended in romance. In the 1938 film *Brother Rat*, he was paired with newcomer Jane Wyman. Wyman had been a dancer in her early movies but later emerged as a bubbly, perky actress. Their dalliance on camera led to dating off the set. Wyman would later say, "I was drawn to him at once. . . . He was such a sunny person."

No Room for Bigotry

Reagan used to say he was the son of a mixed marriage background—an Irish Catholic father and a Scottish Presbyterian mother. Once when his father checked into a hotel, the clerk said, while reading his name, "You'll like it here. We don't permit a Jew in the place."

Jack Reagan picked up his suitcase and said, "I'm a Catholic, and if it's come to the point you won't take Jews, you won't take me either." It was the only hotel in the town, so he spent the night in his car in the snow. He became very ill, and a short time later he had a heart attack, the first of several that would lead to his death.

"Old Man Reagan"

In November 1980, former governor Ronald Reagan was elected president. The fortieth chief executive, at the age of sixty-eight, was the oldest man ever elected, beating out by a few months General William Henry Harrison, elected 140 years earlier. Reagan—notwithstanding his Alzheimer's—lived to age ninety-two, surpassing John Adams as the oldest surviving president. (Adams lived to age ninety.) Reagan's mark, however, would be later topped by former president Gerald Ford, who died in December 2006 at age ninety-three.

One for the Books

After World War II, Reagan returned to acting. His first big movie was *The Hasty Heart*, filmed in postwar London. It was during this time of British Socialist government that Reagan first developed an antipathy for the welfare state.

In *The Hasty Heart*, Reagan had the supporting role, playing Yank next to the lead, British actor Richard Todd. In the script, an English soldier scoffs to the American that he can't name the books of the Bible. The Yank then reels off, "Genesis, Exodus, Leviticus, Numbers, Deuteronomy, Joshua, Judges, Ruth, Samuel, Kings, Chronicles, Ezra, Nehemiah, Esther, Job, Psalms, Proverbs, Ecclesiastes, Solomon, Isaiah, Jeremiah, Lamentations . . ."

Reagan did this in the first take, to the amazement of all. Years later, in the White House, he could still recite all the books of the Bible.

Pain in the Neck?

When the Warner Brothers movie men looked over Reagan's screen test, they shook their heads. "There's a problem with his neck. It's too short."

But another said, "Maybe it can be fixed." He explained, "Jimmy Cagney had the same problem, and we had a shirt maker design shirts that masked the problem." Behind the neck the shirt had the same normal collar band, but as it encircled the neck it became narrower and smaller. The tips of the collar laid flat on his chest, revealing a few more inches of skin that would not have been exposed by a normal collar.

In addition, they told Reagan to stop wearing narrow ties and to use a Windsor knot with an extra-wide collar. He would wear shirts in the same style ever after.

Pennies for Heaven

Maureen Reagan, the child of Ronald Reagan and Jane Wyman, was lonely. She wanted a little brother. She saved up her pennies in her piggy bank. When she had close to two dollars, she went to the drug store and emptied her dollar and ninety-seven cents on the counter. "I want a baby brother."

The disappointed Maureen was turned away, but the pharmacist got word to the Reagan household in Beverly Hills. Her parents discussed it. The problem was that Wyman's doctor, after the difficult delivery of Maureen, advised against another childbirth. So they adopted.

When the baby, who would be named Michael, was brought to the Reagan house in 1945, Maureen emptied her piggy bank and gave the 197 pennies to the nurse.

Play It Again, Ron

Perhaps the greatest movie of all time is *Casablanca*, which came out in 1942. Movie buffs tell the story that Reagan was considered for the role of Rick, the ill-starred lover of Ilsa, played by Ingrid Bergman. Yes, he was considered for that role, along with George Raft, but only briefly. Jack Warner actually had his eye on Reagan to play the role of Victor Laszlo, but eventually opted for Paul Henreid.

The Preacher and the Crooner

When giving a speech before a dinner, Reagan would not eat. But he would order a pot of hot water and two big chocolate chip cookies—the first, he said, to help his vocal chords (hot water, not cold) and the second for quick energy.

He added, "I got these suggestions from an old preacher and crooner." They were Billy Graham and Frank Sinatra.

Presidential Prediction

In Reagan's greatest film, 1942's *Kings Row*, the lead star was Robert Cummings. He was very taken with Reagan's presence and projection of confidence both on and off the set. He said to him, "One day, Ron, I'm going to vote for you for president."

Reagan laughed it off, but Cummings would keep saying it whenever they met in Hollywood. Reagan would say later, "Never in my wildest dreams in those days did I ever consider seeking public office."

Rainbow and Rawhide

The Secret Service code name for Reagan was "Rawhide," and the one for Nancy was "Rainbow." One of the agents assigned to protect them recalled when the First Lady first visited Reagan after the shooting in March 1981, wearing a dress of bright colors. As soon as he saw Rainbow, Rawhide's pale, ashen face lit up at once.

Rock of Ages

On the Reagan Ranch, there is a rock bearing the initials R.W.R. and N.D.R. carved inside a heart. Reagan carved it himself. His children call it the "Heart Rock."

The Rod and Ron

In 1947, Reagan noted the influence of the Communist Party in the Screen Actors Guild. As head of the actors' union, Reagan started to speak out against Stalinism. He received some anonymous calls with threats to hurl acid at his face—to end his acting career—if he continued his speeches against Communism.

Reagan bought a revolver and brought it to the Warner Brothers lot on days he would be giving a talk afterward.

Role Model

Reagan was by profession an actor, and his greatest role was that of president. His first political hero and role model for president was Franklin Roosevelt.

In 1942, the Oscar went to James Cagney for playing George M. Cohan in *Yankee Doodle Dandy*. Reagan always believed that he might have won an Oscar for his role in *Kings Row* but for the fact that Warner Brothers could push for only one of its actors for Oscar that year, and that was Cagney. Reagan saw Cagney's movie many times, and one scene that made an indelible impression was one in which the actor playing FDR presents a medal to Cohan in the White House. The FDR character is warm and outgoing and makes Cohan feel ten feet tall. Cohan leaves dancing down the White House stairs. As president, Reagan made a point of doing the same for his visitors. He wanted to make them feel at ease and proud of their accomplishments.

Romance or Rescue?

Across the country there are many historical plaques honoring heroic acts performed by presidents before they were ever elected to the White House. Most recount battle victories by presidents who were previously generals.

But in Dixon, Illinois, a plaque in the public park attests to the gallantry of a lifeguard, Ronald Wilson Reagan, for his rescuing of seventy-eight women in the large pool.

Nancy was skeptical of the number. She suspected some of the "rescues" might have been spurred more by hopes of romance than by drowning.

A Rose by Any Other Name

Reagan was a radio reporter covering the Chicago Cubs in their spring training camp in Catalina, California, in 1937 when he tried out in Hollywood to fulfill a longtime dream. He was then known as "Dutch," his nickname from boyhood. He did not like the name Ronald.

Those were the days when Hollywood always gave actors more glamorous names. Reagan's future wife, Jane Wyman, was born Sarah Jane Mayfield. His future best man in his second marriage, William Holden, was originally called William Beedle. His future star in *The Winning Team*, Doris Day, was born Doris von Kappelhoff. Fred Austerlitz became Fred Astaire; Leonard Slye was restyled as Roy Rogers.

The movie men said, "You can't put 'Dutch Reagan' on a theater marquee." They then experimented with many names that sounded catchy. Reagan timidly offered, "Why not Ronald Reagan?" The movie men repeated his alliterative name and replied, "Sounds good."

Royal Cousin

Ronald Reagan was informed by *Burke's Peerage* in 1984 that he was a sixth cousin of Queen Elizabeth. He was also descended from Brian Boru, the first king of Ireland.

Shirley Shock?

Ronald Reagan was chosen to co-star with child legend Shirley Temple in her first film as an adult. In *That Hagen Girl* (1947), Temple, age nineteen, forms a romantic attachment to Reagan—fifteen years her senior.

At the sneak preview, when Reagan said to Shirley Temple in one scene, "I love you. Will you marry me?" the audience gasped. They couldn't accept the fact that Shirley Temple was no longer a little girl. The producers deleted the line before releasing it for general distribution.

Shoe Shine

One little-known practice of Reagan's was to switch his shoes twice or even three times a day. He claimed that energy often starts with the feet. A pair of fresh shoes seemed to make him sparkle with new vigor.

Sir Tabby

Reagan's favorite stories in childhood were about King Arthur and the Knights of the Round Table. When his cat had kittens, he named them King Arthur and Sir Galahad.

"Smoke Gets in Your Eyes"

Cigarette advertisements often featured Hollywood stars. Readers of *Collier's*, *Look,* and *Life* on occasion saw Ronald Reagan with a cigarette in his hand in a Chesterfield full-page ad with a line underneath reading "They Satisfy."

But no cigarettes satisfied Reagan; he did not smoke.

"There's a Film in Your Future"

In 1943, Reagan, on leave from military service, played in *This Is the Army* with Joan Leslie. The profits would go to Army relief.

The writer of the musical comedy was Irving Berlin. One day Berlin came up to Reagan and said, "Young man, I've seen some of the rushes—you have a few things to correct. Your voice is too husky. But if you correct that, you might have a future in movies when the war is over."

Reagan thanked him for his kindness and refrained from telling Berlin that he had been making movies since 1937.

"There's a Ford in Your Future"

In 1936, Des Moines sports broadcaster Dutch Reagan tried in vain to cover the Iowa-Michigan game in Ann Arbor. Michigan refused to give its permission. So Reagan did it by monitoring the telegraph of the game. Later all he could remember of it was that Michigan won in a rout, mainly due to the magnificent play of its star center, who seemed to be in on the tackle of every play. His name was Gerry Ford.

Winning Pitch?

In 1952, Reagan played Hall of Fame pitcher Grover Cleveland Alexander in *The Winning Team*, with his wife played by Doris Day. It may not have been his greatest acting performance, but it gave him a line he would repeat often in reference to Nancy. He says in the film to Doris Day, "God must think a lot of me to have given me you."

Courtesy Ronald Reagan Library

6

Reagan's Zingers

★ ★ ★ ★ ★ ★ ★ ★ ★ ★ ★ ★ ★ ★ ★

The stories behind
his most memorable lines

Quick-thinking answers or on-the-spot responses are often said to be the truest sign of intelligence. By such criteria, Reagan would be among the most brilliant presidents.

In recent history, Eisenhower, Ford, and the two Bushes were mediocre at the impromptu zingers. Kennedy would top Clinton, and Reagan edges out Kennedy.

By "zingers" I do not mean the one-liners crafted by speechwriters for the Gridiron Dinner or a National Press Club affair. I mean the truly spontaneous comebacks or responses to questions or events.

Some of Reagan's one-liners were from movie scripts: "Where's the rest of me?"; "Win one for the Gipper." But "I am paying for this microphone" was pure Ronald Reagan. So was "There you go again" (even though he did first say it in the debate rehearsal).

Reagan knew how to spot a zinger, as well as how to coin one, and he used them with an actor's timing and thrust to great effect.

"Are You Happier Today Than When Mr. Carter Became President of the United States?"

In the October 28, 1980, debate with President Jimmy Carter, just a week before the election, Reagan closed with a sort of rhetorical question: "Are you better off than you were four years ago?" Continuing, he asked:

Is our nation stronger and more capable of leading the world toward peace and freedom or is it weaker? Is there more stability in the world or less? Are you convinced that we earned the respect of the world and our allies, or has America's position across the globe diminished? Are you personally more secure in your life? Is your family more secure? Is America safer in the world? And most importantly—quite simply—the basic question of our lives: Are you happier today than when Mr. Carter became president of the United States?

"By the Looks of You, You Don't Look Like You Could Do Much of Either"

In Los Angeles, Governor Reagan marched past protesters as he arrived to speak at the University of California–Los Angeles. The scrawny demonstrators were wearing beads and sandals and were sporting half-baked attempts at beards. Some of their signs proclaimed, "Make love, not war." Reagan stopped and said, "Make love, not war? By the looks of you, you don't look like you could do much of either."

"Let's Go, George. We're Leaving!"

In September 1986, President Reagan journeyed to Reykjavik, Iceland, for a summit conference with Soviet chairman Mikhail Gorbachev. It was the first high-level negotiation with the leaders of the two superpowers in seven years. Expectations were high. The new Soviet chairman, with his programs of *glasnost* and *perestroika*, seemed to manifest a new reform in Russia. It was almost assumed that a treaty limiting missiles would be signed.

Upon his arrival, President Reagan and Secretary of State George Shultz found the Soviet chairman and foreign secretary in a conciliatory mood. The first few days of negotiation went well, but then the Americans discovered that the price for signing the treaty was for the United States to abandon its Strategic Defense Initiative (SDI). The mainstream media had been ridiculing SDI, a billion-dollar program designed to intercept launched missiles, as "Star Wars."

The Soviets had far more confidence in U.S. technological capabilities than the American academic and media establishment did. An exasperated Reagan asked Gorbachev, "If you are willing to abolish nuclear weapons, why are you so anxious to get rid of a defense against nuclear weapons?" But the Soviets insisted on the elimination of SDI. Reagan realized Gorbachev had brought him to Iceland for one purpose—to kill SDI.

Angry, Reagan stood up from the table and turned to Shultz. "Let's go, George," he said. "We're leaving." The American mainstream media savaged Reagan for coming home empty-handed, but Iceland, the host country (not incidentally, the first signatory of NATO), applauded his actions.

"Honey, I Forgot to Duck!"

On March 30, 1981, President Reagan donned a brand-new blue suit to address the Construction Trades Council at the Hilton Hotel in Washington. This was the last time he wore that suit, because a young man named John Hinckley shot him as he left the hotel after his speech. When Reagan suddenly felt a sharp pain in his back, he said to Secret Service agent Jerry Parr, who had pushed him into the waiting limousine, "Jerry, get off. I think you've broken one of my ribs."

The limousine headed straight for George Washington University Hospital as blood frothed up in Reagan's mouth.

He passed out, and when he woke up, his wife was looking down on him. He said, "Honey, I forgot to duck"—a line stolen from Jack Dempsey when he was beaten by Gene Tunney in 1926 for the heavyweight championship.

"I've Got a Story!"

When speaking on what he called the "mashed potato circuit," to set up a startling anecdote or statistic on government waste, Reagan would use a line from his early B movie days with Warner Brothers. He had done eight films about a star reporter, in which he would rush into a room with his hat on the back of his head. Grabbing a phone, he yelled, "Give me the city desk! I've got a story that will crack this town wide open!"

"I Am Paying for This Microphone"

In March 1980, the New Hampshire primary loomed. It was crucial for Ronald Reagan. George H. W. Bush had upset Reagan in the Iowa caucus and came to New Hampshire boasting of the "Big Mo" (momentum).

There were several other candidates, including Senator Bob Dole, Senator Howard Baker, Congressman Jack Kemp, and Congressman John Anderson. But the *Nashua Telegraph*, figuring it was a two-man race, planned to sponsor a one-on-one debate between Bush and Reagan.

Senator Bob Dole complained to the Federal Election Commission that this sponsorship—excluding the lesser candidates—would be an illegal contribution to the Reagan and Bush campaigns. The FEC agreed, and the Reagan team offered to split the cost of the debate, which would include all the other candidates. The Bush team declined to do the same. Reagan's campaign manager, John Sears, called the other Republican candidates and invited them.

Bush, however, refused to share the platform with anyone but Reagan. Although the original ground rules had specified only two candidates, Reagan had told the other candidates he would not appear without them.

Reagan did not want to appear that he was afraid to debate Bush. Followed by the other four candidates, he marched up to a table meant for only two candidates. The crowd soon began agitating for a broader debate, but Bush was clearly opposed to the idea. Reagan took the microphone and began to advocate for a debate among all the candidates. Because the *Telegraph* had invited only two candidates, the paper's editor shouted to sound men to turn off Reagan's microphone. Reagan shot back, "I am paying for this microphone."

He beat Bush right then.

"I Will Not Exploit My Opponent's Youth and Inexperience"

It was the second presidential debate with former vice president Walter Mondale in 1984. Many observers thought Reagan had "lost" his first debate, for which his advisors had over-coached him with too many statistics and programs.

For the second debate, it was decided to let Reagan be Reagan.

One questioner raised the issue of age, referring to a possibly sensitive subject. At age seventy-three, Reagan was the oldest of any serving president.

Reagan's wit turned the question into a winner: "I am not going to exploit for political purposes my opponent's youth and inexperience." Even Mondale was floored, letting out a spontaneous, hearty laugh.

"Mr. Gorbachev, Tear Down This Wall"

In June 1987, Reagan flew to West Berlin. There at the Brandenburg Gate he addressed tens of thousands of Berliners.

Early in his remarks, Reagan said, "Behind me stands a wall that encircles the free sectors of this city, part of a vast system of barriers that divides the entire continent of Europe."

As soon as Mikhail Gorbachev assumed the leadership of the Soviet Union, the Western press hailed him as a new kind of Red dictator, one who was ushering in *glasnost*, which suggested a reaching out to the West. The American and Western European media expected Reagan would be merely conciliatory to the Communist leaders, who were, after all, "moderating." He had different plans.

Speechwriter Peter Hannaford had written a hard-line speech, but the State Department had edited out all unbecoming diplomatic language that might exacerbate tensions.

Although it was not in the text that Reagan held in his hand on that July 12, he kept the hard-line demand anyway.

"General Secretary Gorbachev, if you seek peace, if you seek prosperity for the Soviet Union and Eastern Europe, if you seek liberalization: Come here to this gate! Mr. Gorbachev, open this gate! Mr. Gorbachev, tear down this wall!"

"I Hope You're a Republican"

On the day Reagan was shot, he was taken immediately to George Washington University Hospital. Within a few minutes after the president was rushed into the operating room, the head surgeon said, "Mr. President, we are going to operate on you." Reagan said, "I hope you're a Republican." The doctor replied, "Today, Mr. President, we are all Republicans."

"There's Nothing More Exhilarating Than to Be Shot At Without Result"

From his hospital bed, Reagan penned a note in which he quoted Winston Churchill, who had been shot at in the Afghan mountains in 1896: "There's no more exhilarating feeling than to be shot at without result." Reagan had used the Churchill line in a toast to Prime Minister Margaret Thatcher three months before.

"There You Go Again"

In the 1980 campaign, President Jimmy Carter declined to appear in the first presidential debate with Reagan and independent candidate Congressman John Anderson. The second debate was a two-way affair between Carter and Reagan. In the rehearsal, David Stockman (Reagan's future budget director) played Carter. He was relentless; Reagan would later say that after Stockman, Carter was easy.

At one point in the rehearsals, Stockman ripped Reagan apart on nuclear proliferation. In a post-mortem consensus from the campaign team, Reagan was less than spectacular. At this point, Reagan said, "I was about to say to Carter (Stockman), 'There you go again,' but I wanted to save it for the debate." And Reagan did, after Carter launched a litany of charges against Reagan's position on health programs. With a cock of his head and a few rueful shakes, Reagan said, "There you go again." It deflected and defeated Carter.

"Where's the Rest of Me?"

Kings Row, released in 1942, was the only movie for which there was any talk of Ronald Reagan winning an Academy Award. However, Warner Brothers had also made *Yankee Doodle Dandy* with James Cagney that year. In those years, the studio usually got behind only one picture in the Oscar race. A New York critic said of Reagan's role, "It will give you that rare glow which comes from seeing a job crisply done, competently and with confidence."

In the film, Reagan's character, Drake McHugh, has his legs amputated by a sadistic surgeon (Charles Coburn). McHugh awakens from the operation and cries, "Where's the rest of me?"

It would be the title of Reagan's first autobiography, published in 1965, and he frequently alluded to the line in talks.

"Win One for the Gipper"

As Reagan once said, "Until I got the part of George Gipp in *Knute Rockne: All American*, I was the Errol Flynn of the B pictures. I usually played a jet-propelled newspaperman who solved more crimes than a polygraph machine."

Reagan had always been fascinated with the life of Rockne, the Notre Dame football coach who died in a plane crash in 1931. He approached a fellow Irishman, Pat O'Brien, to play the part of Rockne.

In the 1940 film, Gipp dies as a young man. Just before dying, he tells Rockne, "Some day, when things are tough and the breaks are going bad for the boys, ask them to go out and win one for the Gipper." Rockne would later tell this to his team, and the Irish came from behind to win the game.

Reagan became nicknamed "the Gipper" by some, and he later told the story to rally the Republican faithful.

© David Hume Kennerly/Getty Images

7

Reagan's Yarns and Tales

* * * * * * * * * * * * * * * * * *

Entertaining stories by and about the man

The White House may never have been home to a raconteur equal to Ronald Reagan. Abraham Lincoln was the first accomplished storyteller in the Oval Office. Like Lincoln, Reagan's funny yarns were a shield to deflect any intimacy. For Lincoln, they were a mask for his melancholy; for Reagan they made a charming and colorful wall put up to prevent anyone from getting too close. Reagan's only real friend and confidante was his wife, Nancy.

To some, like Secretary of State Alexander Haig and Speaker Tip O'Neill, this bottomless well of anecdotes signaled a lack of knowledge or serious purpose. But Reagan, like Lincoln, had his principles and goals firmly set. Reagan did not enjoy the company of politicians. For relaxation and escape, he much preferred talking with movie people about old Hollywood days.

Unlike any previous president, Reagan had a filed collection of stories on 5 x 8 cards. He used them in speeches to illustrate points or outline messages. After he told a story, he never told it in that city again (just as his wife would never wear the same dress twice in any city). When Reagan told a story for a national television audience, he would rip it up and never use it again.

The Great Communicator, like the Great Emancipator before him, was a master of advocacy by amusement.

Backside Boss

At Moscow University in 1988, President Reagan spun this folk tale. In a dig at bureaucracies, he told of a woman who accosted a functionary at a meeting, telling him:

There is a folk legend here where I come from that when a baby is born, an angel comes down from heaven and kisses it on one part of the body. If the angel kisses him on his hand he becomes a handyman. If he kisses him on his forehead he becomes bright and clever. And I've been trying to figure where the angel kissed you that you should sit there for so long and do nothing.

The Moscow students laughed uproariously.

Bearing Down

Reagan liked to use the analogy of two hikers who wake up from their campsite to see a grizzly bear approaching. One camper dives into his knapsack and pulls out a pair of sneakers. As he takes off his boots to put on the sneakers, his companion says, "You know you can't outrun a grizzly." His companion replies, "I know. I just have to outrun you."

Big Bang Theory

Reagan told this story to poke fun at the economic pundits who predicted his fiscal policies, which they scornfully labeled "Reaganomics," would lead the country to a disaster:

It seems a surgeon, an engineer, and an economist were arguing over which was the oldest profession. The doctor said, "It was medicine, because it was a surgeon who took the rib from Adam to make Eve." "No," answered the engineer, "because it was an engineer who brought order out of chaos."

But the economist had the final word. He declared, "But surely it was the economist who caused the chaos!"

Big Brother Watching?

Reagan liked to retell a story he heard from Mikhail Gorbachev about Leonid Brezhnev, one of Gorbachev's predecessors. The son of poor peasants, Brezhnev had risen to become Soviet chairman. Proud of his new station, with the trappings of power that would have pleased a czar, he brought his aged mother in a huge limousine from her village to the Kremlin and showed her his fabulously appointed apartment.

Afterward he had the limousine take them to his country place in the woods outside Moscow. Following that, they took a train to the Crimea, where Brezhnev had a marble palace on the beach. Astonished, his mother whispered in his ear, "Leonid, what if the Communists found out?"

Busy Signal

A senior Democratic senator came to the Oval Office to protest the president's position on lowering tariffs, which he believed would cause unemployment in his state, as jobs would be lost to foreign manufacturers.

Reagan sighed and expressed his appreciation of the senator's concerns, but he remained firm to the cause of freer trade and the resulting economic growth.

The distraught senator left, saying, "I'm going out of here and doing some praying." Reagan replied, "Well, if you get a busy signal, it's me there ahead of you!"

Cabbage Complexity

In 1982, as Reagan was pushing for reform and simplification of American regulatory codes, he liked to cite an item he read in a Toledo small business journal:

It is reported to us that the Lord's Prayer contains 57 words. Lincoln's Gettysburg Address has 266 words. The Ten Commandments are presented in just 297 words, and the Declaration of Independence has only 300 words. An Agriculture Department order setting the price of cabbage has 26,911 words.

Clap Trap?

At the 1976 Republican convention in Kansas City, the campaign manager persuaded Reagan to announce that his choice for running mate would be Dick Schweiker, a modest Republican from Pennsylvania. It was an attempt to break up that state's solid seventy-plus votes for Ford. But the pick didn't please everyone.

Reagan invited Schweiker to join him as he visited some Southern delegations for votes. At the Alabama delegation, a delegate rose and said:

Gov'ner, I don't know how you could have picked this fella. Ah'm not a drinkin' man, but the night I heard you picked Schweiker I went home and drank a whole pitcher of whiskey sours. I would rather my doctor had told me my wife had a dose of the clap.

Damn Yankee!

Often when Reagan spoke on behalf of General Electric, he would come on stage to the musical accompaniment of "The Battle Hymn of the Republic," not the most popular song in the South. Once in Alabama, Reagan was to be introduced by a local GE manager, a Yankee transfer to Dixie. As he was about to begin his spiel, a good ol' boy in the front asked, "What's going to be the subject of Reagan's talk?"

The introducer (a bit of a card) said with a straight face, "It's entitled 'Robert E. Lee: a traitor to his country.'"

Reagan had a hard time extracting himself from that introduction.

Dead-Set Democrat

In a 1973 Chicago speech, Governor Reagan said, "As you know, I grew up in Dixon, Illinois, and had relatives in Chicago. All of us in my whole family were Democrats. As a matter of fact, I had an uncle in Chicago who won a medal for never having missed voting in an election for fifteen years—and he had been dead for fourteen."

Demand and Supply?

Ronald Reagan was not an indulgent father. Michael Reagan still complains about his dollar-a-week allowance compared to the weekly haul children of Beverly Hills stars like Joan Crawford and Bob Hope received.

One Saturday Michael cornered his father and dared to ask him for more money. Instead of an extra dollar, he got a discourse on economics, the U.S. tax code, and his father's expenses with a new wife and new child.

But eventually Reagan relented and said, "Michael, if a president is elected who cuts taxes, I'll give you a raise."

When John F. Kennedy cut taxes in 1961, Reagan kept his promise. As Michael now tells it, his allowance was upped to $5.00.

Dog Gone!

One of Reagan's closest friends was Lucky, a Belgian sheepdog who was often at the president's side in the Oval Office. Lucky drove some of the president's staff nuts; they were trying to talk to him while he was trying to train the new puppy.

One day Michael Deaver said, "Mr. President, you need to get that dog out of here. He's going to end up pissing on your desk."

Reagan looked up and said, "Why not? Everyone else does."

Dog Gone?

In 1984, Charles Schultz's comic strip *Peanuts* had Snoopy the beagle considering a run for the presidency. Reagan wrote Schultz, a friend and fellow Californian, a letter of mock worry: "Anything you can do to talk Snoopy out of it would be appreciated. How would he feel about a cabinet position?"

Doggone Great!

During the Iran-Contra affair, Reagan told this story to the Conservative Political Action Conference:

You know, these last several weeks, I've felt a little bit like that farmer that was driving his horse and wagon to town for some grain and had a head-on collision with a truck. And later was the litigation involving claims for his injuries, some of them permanent.

And he was on the stand and a lawyer said to him, "Isn't it true that while you were lying there at the scene of the accident someone came over to you and asked you how you were feeling, and you said you never felt better in your life?"

And he said, "Yes, I remember that." Well, later he's on the stand and the witnesses were there—the lawyer for the other side is questioning—and he said, "When you gave that answer about how you felt, what were the circumstances?"

"Well," he said, "I was lying there and a car came up and a deputy sheriff got out. My horse was screaming with pain—had broken two legs. The deputy took out his gun, put it in the horse's ear, and finished him off.

"And my dog was whining with pain—had a broken back. He went over to him and put the gun in his ear.

"And then, he turned to me and says, 'How are you feeling?'"

DUI—Drinking Under the Influence?

Another Reagan story touched on the topic of false hospitality.

Two cars collide in a head-on crash. The driver of one car is a farmer. In the other smashed car is a lawyer. The farmer says to the attorney, "You look pretty shaken up. Stay right there. I got something for you." The farmer goes back to his car and pulls out a flask from the glove compartment. He offers it to the lawyer. "Take a swig."

The lawyer does, and the farmer says, "You better have another." The lawyer takes another gulp. "Feel better now? You better have one more."

"Yes!" says the attorney. "Don't you want some too?"

"No," replied the farmer. "I'm just waiting for the state trooper to arrive."

Duty Calls

In 1975, Reagan asked his friend and advisor Michael Deaver if he should run against President Ford for the presidency. Deaver told him Ford couldn't win but that he could. There was no one better than he at communicating ideals and principles to the American people.

Reagan nodded and said, "I remember in the movie *Santa Fe Trail*, I was playing a lieutenant to a wounded captain who was portrayed by Errol Flynn. The captain said, 'You got to take over.' And I said, 'I can't.' And the captain said, 'But it's your duty.'"

Em–bra–assing!

In 1946, Reagan was in London after filming *The Hasty Heart* with Richard Todd and Patricia Neal. One Warner Brothers representative in London was married to an English girl. Joined by Reagan, the three decided to go to the Riviera for the weekend, take the channel ferry back to England, and then hop the train to Southampton. The American's wife discovered she had left her passport back in the hotel, so the two men boarded the ferry without her. The female French customs inspector asked Reagan to open the bags. The first suitcase belonged to the missing woman. As she went through the very feminine bag, the inspector pulled out panties and bras. She turned to Reagan and said, "*Tres jolie.*"

Forgettable Fritz

In Reagan's campaign for re-election in 1984, the Democratic presidential candidate, former vice president Walter "Fritz" Mondale, constantly referred to the president's advanced age. At that time Reagan was the oldest man to serve in the White House. On one occasion, Mondale charged that Reagan ran a government by amnesia.

With his customary wit, Reagan disarmed his opponents: "I thought that remark accusing me of amnesia was uncalled for. I just wish I could remember who said it."

Foul Play?

In 1934, when "Dutch" Reagan was announcing Chicago Cubs games from Des Moines by wire telegraph, he had perfected the skill of describing the game just as if he were sitting in Wrigley Field.

One afternoon he was handed a more difficult challenge. The power went off as Cubs shortstop Billy Jurges faced off against Dizzy Dean. The quick-thinking Reagan improvised. As he told it:

There were several other stations broadcasting that game, and I knew I'd lose my audience if I told them we'd lost our telegraph connections, so I took a chance. I had Jurges hit another foul. Then I had him foul one that only missed being a home run by a foot. I had him foul one back in the stands and took up some time describing the two lads that got in a fight over the ball. I kept on having him foul balls until I was setting a record for a ballplayer hitting successive foul balls and I was getting more than a little scared. Just then my operator started typing. When he passed me the paper I started to giggle— it said "Jurges popped out on the first ball pitched."

From Princes to Presidents

One March President Reagan went into the Rose Garden to greet the arriving president of Venezuela. He pulled the prepared remarks from his overcoat pocket to deliver. When he looked down, the words in front of him were generous praise for the enlightened leadership of the Grand Duke of Luxembourg. Reagan quickly had to shift gears from Luxembourg to Latin America and from a prince to a president.

Generation Gap

In 1969, when college campuses erupted in protest of the Vietnam War, student leaders from the nine University of California campuses asked to see Governor Reagan in Sacramento.

The delegation arrived in the capitol; most of them were barefoot and wore torn T-shirts. When Governor Reagan entered his office, they were sprawled out on the floor. None of them stood up.

Then their spokesman began speaking. "Governor, we want to talk to you, but I think you should realize that it's impossible for you to understand us. It's sad, but it's impossible for the members of your generation to understand your own children. You weren't raised in a time of instant communications or satellites and computers solving problems in seconds that previously took hours or days or even weeks to solve. You didn't live in an age of space travel and journeys to the moon, of jet travel or high-speed electronics."

As the spokesman paused for breath, Reagan said, "You're absolutely right. We didn't have those things when we were your age. We invented them."

Grave Undertaking?

Fellow Illinoisan Abraham Lincoln was Reagan's greatest hero, and his favorite Lincoln story involved presidential patronage. It was an anecdote he used to tell audiences across America in the 1950s, when he—next to President Eisenhower—was the public speaker most in demand. In discussions of bureaucracy, Reagan told of a government job-seeker who learned that a member of the Customs Office had just died.

The job-seeker came rushing into the White House and said, "President Lincoln, can I take his place?"

Lincoln paused and said, "Yes, I suppose you can—if it's all right with the undertaker."

Horse "Scents"

Reagan was a great raconteur, but not all his anecdotes could pass a lie detector test. One tale he told took place at Windsor Castle, where he stayed on a state visit in 1982.

Like Reagan, Queen Elizabeth was a great equestrian, and the two took a ride together on the castle grounds. Her Majesty's steed—suffering perhaps from some stale oats—began to expel gas rhythmically with each step. Elizabeth, by the grace of God Queen of Great Britain, Defender of the Faith, was a bit embarrassed and said, "Oh dear, Mr. President, I'm so sorry!"

Reagan replied, "Quite all right, Your Majesty. I thought it was the horse."

Hot Seats?

In the spring of 1985, President Reagan took a trip to Europe. One of the countries he visited was Portugal. On this state visit, he was invited to address the assembly in Lisbon. Just as he began his remarks, the Communist members made a show of walking out. Reagan then quipped, "I'm sorry that some of the chairs on the left seem to be uncomfortable."

Hot Enough for You?

One of Reagan's favorite stories was about the shortest sermon he had ever heard. In Dixon, Illinois, one August Sunday, it was so hot, he said, that you could have fried an egg on the steps up to the wooden white church. As the family suffered through the service, they dreaded the upcoming long sermon. When the preacher stepped to the pulpit, he simply pointed down and said, "It's hotter Down There." And that was it.

If You Ask a Stupid Question...

At a Young Presidents' Organization conference in Arizona in 1976, Reagan was questioned by three panelists. At that time Reagan was running for president against the Republican incumbent, President Gerald Ford. One panelist from the East was working for Ford and thought Reagan too shallow for the office of president.

To expose Reagan's superficiality, he asked, "What are your thoughts on the intrinsic moral capability of man?"

In his reply, Reagan did not directly answer but talked about individual responsibility and then answered some other panelists' questions. When it came the hostile panelist's turn again, he said, "Mr. Reagan, I didn't understand the answer to my question." "Young man," answered Reagan, "I didn't understand your question."

Lighting a Candle

A story that Reagan could not tell without tearing up involved an encounter in 1984 with the former ambassador from Poland, who had defected.

The former diplomat had one message: "Mr. President, never let Radio Free Europe go off the air. You have no idea what it meant to hear the chimes of Big Ben from the BBC in London during World War II."

Then the Pole said, "May I ask you a favor? Mr. President, would you light a candle and put it in the window tonight for the people of Poland?" And right then, Reagan got up and went to the second floor, lit a candle, and put it in a window.

"Likewise, I'm Sure"

On one occasion, Reagan told Mikhail Gorbachev about an American and a Russian who were arguing about their two countries.

The American said, "Look, I can go into the Oval Office, pound the president's desk, and say, 'Mr. President, I don't like the way you're running the country.'"

And the Russian replied, "I can do that too."

"You can?" the American asked.

The Russian replied, "Sure. I can go into the Kremlin into the general secretary's office and say, 'Mr. General Secretary, I don't like the way President Reagan is running his country.'"

The Little Red Hen

Reagan loved parables—stories that exemplified a principle or archetype. On the speech circuit in the 1950s, one he often told was called "The Modern Little Red Hen."

Once upon a time, there was a little red hen who scratched around the barnyard until she uncovered some grains of wheat. She called her neighbors and said, "If we plant this wheat, we shall have bread to eat. Who will help me reap my wheat?"

"Not I," said the duck.

"Out of my classification," said the pig.

"I'd lose my seniority," said the cow.

"I'd lose my unemployment compensation," said the goose.

"Then I will," said the little red hen, and she did.

At last, it came time to bake the bread.

"Who will help me bake bread?" asked the little red hen.

"That would be overtime for me," said the cow.

"I'd lose my welfare benefits," said the duck.

"I'm a dropout and never learned how," said the pig.

"If I'm only to be a helper, that's discrimination," said the goose.

"Then I will," said the little red hen.

She baked five loaves and held them up for her neighbors to see. They all wanted some, and in fact, demanded a share. But the little red hen said,

"No. I can eat the five loaves myself."

"Excess profit!" cried the cow.

"Capitalist leech!" screamed the duck.

"I demand equal rights!" yelled the goose.

And they all painted picket signs and marched around the little red hen shouting obscenities. When the government agent came, he said to the little red hen, "You must not be greedy."

"But I earned the bread," she said.

"Exactly. That's the wonderful free enterprise system. Anyone in the barnyard can earn as much as he wants, but under our modern government regulation, the productive workers must divide their product with the idle."

And they lived happily ever after. But her neighbors wondered why she never baked any more bread.

Lucky Duck

One story Reagan told to staffers on a bus in New Hampshire in 1980 got him into hot water. He said, "How do you tell the Polish one at a cockfight?" The answer: "He's the one with a duck."

"And how do you tell the Italian one? He's the one who bets on the duck."

Then he added, "And how do you know the Mafia is there?" Reagan raised his voice and said, "The duck wins." Reagan had a lot of explaining to do to some Italian American groups after that.

Matching Actions with Words

Reagan asked a Republican senator to visit him in the Oval Office. Reagan needed him on a trade vote, but the lawmaker cited constituent pressure against imports. The senator said, "Mr. President, there is no one who admires you more than I do. Why, I'd jump out of an airplane without a parachute if you said 'jump,' but. . ."

And then Reagan leaned forward and said, "Jump!"

The senator changed his vote.

Mayor and the Monkey

Ronald Reagan was not the only Hollywood actor to co-star with a monkey (*Bedtime for Bonzo*). Clint Eastwood appeared in two films (*Every Which Way but Loose* and *Any Which Way You Can*) with an orangutan. In 1986, when President Reagan heard that Eastwood was elected mayor of Carmel, California, President Reagan told him, "What makes you think that a middle-aged movie actor who's played with a chimp could have a future in politics?"

Mea Culpa

In 1982, ABC White House correspondent Sam Donaldson challenged the president at a news conference. "Mr. President, I'm talking about the continuing recession," piped up Donaldson. "You have blamed others for the mistakes of the past. Doesn't any of the blame belong to you?"

"Yes," replied Reagan, "because for many years I was a Democrat."

A Million Movies?

In a cabinet meeting in 1982, the secretary of agriculture informed the president that 478 million pounds of surplus butter had been located in storage. Reagan quipped, "Does anyone know where we can find 478 million pounds of popcorn?"

Muddying the Field

Whenever politicians and the media engaged in finger-pointing and blaming their predecessors, Reagan would trot out this Frankie Frisch story. Frisch, the "Fordham Flash" (unlike most baseball players of his day, he had graduated from college), became a Hall of Famer. The fiery shortstop was the player-manager of the 1934 World Series champion St. Louis Cardinals, nicknamed the "Gas House Gang."

In 1981 Reagan told the story this way:

One day the great baseball manager Frankie Frisch sent a rookie out to play center field. The rookie promptly dropped the first fly ball that was hit to him.

On the next play he let a grounder go between his feet and then threw the ball to the wrong base. Frankie stormed out of the dugout, took his glove away from him, and said, "I'll show you how to play this position." And the next batter slammed a line drive right over second base. Frankie came in on it, missed it completely, fell down when he tried to chase it, threw down his glove, and yelled at the rookie, "You've got center field so screwed up nobody can play it."

One Potato, Two Potato…

To a group of Cuban Americans in Florida, Reagan recounted a folk story Soviet people were passing around about a Soviet commissar who went to inspect one of the collective farms:

He stopped the first farmer, workman that he met, and he asked about life on the farm. And the man said, "It's wonderful. I've never heard anyone complain about anything since I've been here."

And the commissar then said, "Well, what about the crops?"

"Oh," he said, "the crops are wonderful."

"What about the potatoes?"

"Oh, sir," he said, "the potatoes," he said, "there are so many that if we put them in one pile they would touch the foot of God."

And the commissar said, "Just a minute. In the Soviet Union there is no God."

And the farmer said, "Well, there are no potatoes either."

Playing Footsie

In 1939, Ronald Reagan had a supporting role as the soldier buddy of Errol Flynn in *Santa Fe Trail*. Others had parts larger than his, including Olivia de Havilland, Raymond Massey, Ward Bond, and Van Heflin.

In one of the publicity shots Reagan was to stand next to Flynn, both in full cowboy regalia with pistols at the ready. Errol Flynn was the studio's swashbuckling leading man and Reagan was only just starting out. Reagan knew he was a better actor than Flynn, not to mention a superior rider. Reagan thought he had a future as a lead in cowboy pictures. He was, however, two inches shorter than Flynn.

As they waited for the photographer, Reagan engaged Flynn in talking—all the while kicking up turf with his foot. When the cameraman came, Reagan had two inches of dirt to stand on, making him as tall as Flynn. Reagan loved to regale his Hollywood friends with this story.

The Preacher and the Politician

To his cabinet, Reagan told a story about an evangelical minister and a politician who died at the same time. They were both greeted at the pearly gates by Saint Peter. Peter showed the preacher his new quarters—a small single room with only furniture a narrow bed and a small table. Then Peter showed the politician his new digs—a palatial mansion of many rooms with long green lawns in front. The politician was a bit confused. "This is for me," he stammered, "after what you showed the preacher?" Peter replied, "You have to understand, we get thousands and thousands of clergy, but you're the first politician in an eon to make it."

A Queer Sight

President Reagan and Queen Elizabeth immediately clicked on Reagan's state visit to Britain in 1982. But Reagan also gained another royal admirer: the Queen Mother.

At a dinner in Windsor Palace—though the two were sitting four places away from each other—they discovered they shared a mutual love of American poet Robert Service.

The two began to recite "The Cremation of Sam McGee." At the end, they were almost shouting the closing refrain:

> The Northern Lights have seen queer sights,
> But the queerest they ever did see
> Was that night on the marge of Lake Lebarge
> I cremated Sam McGee.

Red-Faced Ronnie

Reagan once told of a time when he was governor and was invited to Mexico City for an address. After his speech he received scattered, unenthusiastic applause.

I was a bit embarrassed—but even more so when the next speaker, a representative of the Mexican government, spoke in Spanish. But he was interrupted by applause, by virtually every other line, with the most enthusiastic kind of applause. Now I don't understand Spanish, but to hide the fact, I started clapping too and at the end I clapped longer than anyone else until the American ambassador leaned over to me and said, "I wouldn't do that if I were you. He's interpreting your speech."

Running Foul

The *Washington Post*, never a fan of President Reagan's administration, was not happy with Reagan's announcement of his candidacy for re-election. Shortly thereafter, Reagan held up an article from the newspaper and said, "The other day the *Washington Post* ran a story heralding the return of spring, and I thought it was just another one of the reports on the political campaign. The headline said, 'The Sap Is Running Again.'"

Run Over?

Reagan left the White House in January 1989 as the most popular president in years and as the first two-term chief executive since General Eisenhower to maintain such popularity. Willie Brown, the Democratic Speaker in the California House, proposed to rename a California highway (which the governor had frequently traveled on his way to Sacramento) the Ronald Reagan Freeway.

In a letter to Brown, Reagan thanked him for his generous support and added, "I'll admit that while people have tried their best to drive over me for years, this is the first time I will actively welcome it."

Second Fiddle

During the thawing of the Cold War, Mikhail Gorbachev was lionized by the mainstream media. Credit for the Berlin Wall's destruction and the withdrawal of Russian troops from the former Eastern European satellite countries was given to the benign peace policies of this great world leader. Little praise was given to President Reagan, whose commitment to a strengthened missile system and the proposed Strategic Defense Initiative had truly effected the Soviet Union's collapse.

In 1989, when *Time* magazine named Gorbachev the Man of the Decade, a reporter asked Reagan if he minded being upstaged. "Good lord, no," Reagan responded "I once co-starred with Errol Flynn."

Second Opinion?

When the Office of Management and Budget projected that Reagan's tax cuts would cause a huge spike in the deficit, the president said he felt sympathy for the climber in the mountains of California whose footing had slipped. He found himself falling off the cliff. Not usually a particularly religious man, he yelled toward the sky, "Oh Lord, help me, help me!" A deep voice thundered down from the clouds, "You're on your own." After a pause, the rapidly descending man shouted, "Is there someone else up there I can talk to?"

Seeing Is Believing

On his second day in George Washington University Hospital after being shot, President Reagan was in considerable discomfort. The doctors had put a tube in his throat, the tranquilizers they had given him the night before were wearing off, and he was having trouble breathing. He scribbled a note for the nurses: "Send me to Los Angeles, where I can see the air I'm breathing!"

Set Your Clock Ahead!

Despite their strong partisan differences, Republican President Reagan and Democratic Speaker of the House Tip O'Neill developed a working friendship. O'Neill would come over to the White House to discuss his opposition to certain bills Reagan supported. Then at six o'clock, the two old Irish politicians would swap stories over drinks. Tip used to say, as he objected vigorously to one of Reagan's projects, "That's politics, Mr. President. After six, we can be friends. Before six, it's politics."

One time Reagan tried to end a political fight prematurely by saying, as he fiddled with his watch, "Look, Tip, I'm resetting the watch."

Shoot Suit?

When Reagan was shot, his children were not allowed to visit at first. When Reagan's son Michael was allowed to visit, he found his father looking wan and pale. The president motioned for him to come closer to the bedside.

"Michael, let me give you this advice," he said. "If you're going to be shot, don't wear a new suit."

"But Dad," his son responded, "that doesn't make sense. I mean, how would you . . ."

"Well, I had this new blue suit—never wore it. Look at it over there—they had to rip it off me. I was looking forward to wearing that new blue suit. Now remember, don't wear a new suit if you're going to get shot."

Sliding into First

On the suggestion of a friend, Ronald Reagan called Nancy Davis and asked her to go out to dinner with him. Nancy discovered after she answered the doorbell that her blind date was also a lame date. Reagan had arrived at her step on crutches.

Then she recalled a recent news story headlined, "Reagan Hurt Sliding into First Base," about a charity softball game Hollywood actors had organized.

"You got yourself hurt, I understand, sliding into first?" she asked.

"No," an embarrassed Reagan explained. "Anybody that knows a thing about baseball knows you never slide into first base—people out in the country must think me an idiot. What happened was that Bob Hope was pitching. I bunted the ball. And the first baseman was blocking the bag, and I tripped and somehow broke my leg."

Though the first moments were awkward, when the dinner at La Rue ended that night Nancy knew that this was the first man she ever met whom she wanted to marry and that he was going to be first in her life ever after.

Star Struck

On the Fourth of July in 1924, in Dixon, Illinois, twelve-year-old Ronald Reagan had a great time with a friend watching fireworks and then going on some daredevil drives. In high spirit at eleven o'clock, Reagan started on his two-mile journey home. A car slowly moseying by stopped and told Reagan to get in as the driver flashed a star on a badge.

Insouciantly Reagan sassed, "Twinkle, twinkle, little star, who the hell do you think you are?" The county sheriff slapped handcuffs on his wrists and took him down to the station house. The sheriff called Ron's father, whom he knew. An irate Jack Reagan came down and paid the $14.50 fine to set his son free.

Time Sharing?

Reagan had a repertoire of stories about the workings of socialism that dated from his days as a spokesman for General Electric.

One was about a man who went to the Soviet Bureau of Transportation to order an automobile. He was told to put his money down even though there was a ten-year wait. Nevertheless, he filled out the various forms and had them processed to the various agencies, and he signed his name in countless places. Finally he got to the last agency, where they put a stamp on his papers. He gave them the money, and they said, "Come back in ten years to get your car." He asked, "Morning or afternoon?" They said, "What difference does it make? We're talking about ten years from now." The man answered, "You see, the plumber is coming in the morning."

Unbearable

In a cabinet meeting early in his presidency, Reagan's cabinet officers were trying to convince him to sign an executive order allowing more economic activity close to wilderness areas. Reagan showed signs of opposing the order, concerned about pollution near the animal sanctuaries.

Energy Secretary Jim Edwards said, "Mr. President, I still don't understand why bears need cleaner air to breathe than us humans."

Edwards won some chuckles with that line, but Reagan shot back, "Jim, have you ever smelled a bear?"

Unsuitable

Reagan may have made the best-dressed list, but his wife had the deeper interest in clothes. One example of Reagan's sartorial apathy was his beloved old topcoat, which Detective Columbo would have retired to the ash heap.

In one of their trips to London, Nancy engaged an English tailor to make her husband a new suit. The small blue-and-gray fabric swatch looked splendid, but some patterns can backfire when they are expanded into a full-size suit.

When the suit arrived at the White House, Nancy and Reagan aide Michael Deaver were aghast. Reagan, however, loved it, and he wore it and wore it and wore it, to Deaver and Mrs. Reagan's dismay.

One day the president asked Deaver, "Mike, what do you think of this suit?"

"Well," replied Deaver, "to be honest, if you had to be shot, why couldn't you have been wearing this suit?"

V.I.P.

When a visitor to the Oval Office would bring up the name of Soviet chairman Mikhail Gorbachev, Reagan would often regale his audience with a story the Soviet leader told him. It seems on one occasion that Gorbachev had lost track of time, and he had to quickly return to the Kremlin for a meeting. "The Moscow speed limits will have to be ignored," said Gorbachev. The driver demurred, saying that under new orders police were stopping everybody.

Gorbachev said, "All right. I'll drive." And he got into the front seat with the chauffeur behind him. As the limo tore down the road past a police car, one policeman said to his partner, "Why didn't you stop him?"

"I do not know who was in the car," the other answered. "He must have been powerfully important, because Gorbachev was his driver!"

World War III

In 1974, Reagan did not run for a third term as governor of California. He had always intended to run in 1976, when President Nixon would have finished his two terms, and the election would be open. Nixon's resignation in the wake of Watergate and Gerald Ford's elevation to the presidency put Reagan in a quandary. He did not relish running against an incumbent president. On the other hand, he regarded Ford as an accidental president who did not reflect the rising surge of conservatism in the Republican Party. He made the decision to run. The eight-year governor knew he had to refurbish his foreign policy credentials to run against Ford.

In 1975 he accepted an invitation to speak to the prestigious forum of the World Affairs Council of Philadelphia, which had hosted many aspiring presidential candidates. The original draft of Reagan's speech—crafted in a think tank—was a stilted academic discourse. Reagan handed the draft to a former White House speechwriter[*] to translate the bureaucratic talk on the Third World.

The "Third World" was mentioned three times in the speech, but each time Reagan would slip up and add another word: "We must address ourselves to the needs of the Third World War."

---

[*] This author was the speechwriter. Reagan spoke in the Bellevue Stratford in March 1975; I sat next to Senator Dick Schweiker and former ambassador to Britain Walter Annenberg.

Women in White

In the 1960s, as a spokesman for General Electric, Reagan made speeches across the country, including many appearances at company plants. In Owensboro, Kentucky, he faced some five thousand women—General Electric's "ladies in white." They were called that because they wore sterile nylon gowns and caps as they made electronic tubes.

When it came time to ask questions, one woman asked, "How do you all like Owensboro?"

"Fine!" answered Reagan. "How can I complain about being here with five thousand girls? Just think, next week I'm in Pittsfield, Massachusetts, where there are thirteen thousand men."

One woman in the middle of the crowd drawled, "You stay here and we'll go to Pittsfield."

The Yolk's on Them

Reagan enjoyed telling the story of a friend who was invited to a costume ball in Washington but didn't have a costume.

So he slapped egg on his face and went. When people asked him who he was supposed to be, he replied, "A liberal economist."

Courtesy Ronald Reagan Library

8

Reagan's Speeches

★ ★ ★ ★ ★ ★ ★ ★ ★ ★ ★ ★ ★ ★ ★ ★

His greatest orations examined

It is often said that Reagan could write better speeches than his speechwriters—and his speechwriters freely admitted it. White House writers were mainly former journalists and reporters who, through training, wrote more for the eye than the ear. For many years Reagan had written his own scripts for radio as well as his talks on the American speech circuit. In other words, he had more experience writing speeches than the speechwriters.

Reagan was a consummate professional in front of the microphone. He made it look easy. His words did not have the cadence of Churchill's stately rhetoric; instead, their conversational style was designed to win over the audience.

He once said that he never uttered words like John F. Kennedy's famous "Ask not what your country can do . . . ," instead sacrificing quotability for credibility. In writing out his drafts, he would imagine himself talking to his barber in Santa Barbara. Scriptwriters will tell you how difficult it is to devise a dialogue line that sounds both powerful and natural.

Reagan, of course, did use writers during his presidency; the demands of the chief executive's role require it. However, Reagan never had an alter ego in his bullpen the way JFK did with Ted Sorensen, Richard Nixon with Ray Price, or George W. Bush with Michael Gerson. Reagan's relationship with his writers was remote, not intimate. White House writers used to say Nixon corrected for substance, Reagan for style, and neither Bush Sr. nor Ford changed a word.

Reagan was indeed the Great Communicator. He mastered the medium of television just as his hero, Franklin D. Roosevelt, had mastered the radio. Like FDR, Reagan manifested both the presence and authority to sell his beliefs and principles, synthesizing the disparate styles of hard-hitting Tony Dolan, philosophical Josh Gilder, and lyrical Peggy Noonan with his unique delivery.

Those who doubt Reagan's ability must read "A Time for Choosing" (1964), which ranks with William Jennings Bryan's "Cross of Gold" (1896) as one of the greatest campaign speeches in history.

Reagan's Washington Debut: Combating Communism

OCTOBER 23, 1947

Reagan's hero was Franklin D. Roosevelt. For most of his acting career, he was a hard-core Democrat, believing that government could solve most economic problems. Right after World War II, Reagan and a fellow Screen Actors Guild member began to lecture about the rise of neo-fascism. Reagan came to realize that the real threat of dictatorship was being manifested in Communism. His speaking out against Communism triggered anonymous threats of violence.

In 1947, he was subpoenaed by the House Un-American Activities Committee to testify about the Communist Party's influence in Hollywood. Reagan had joined a group called the Hollywood Independent Citizens' Committee of the Arts, Sciences and Professions, a respected liberal organization supporting President Roosevelt. But Reagan and a few others, including Jimmy Roosevelt and Olivia de Havilland, realized that it was being taken over by Communists.

The House Un-American Activities Committee, chaired by J. Parnell Thomas, asked actors Robert Taylor, George Murphy, and Reagan to give their statements. To the chairman's disappointment, Reagan refused to disclose the names of those he thought were Communist. After he answered the congress-men's questions, he closed with this statement:

Sir, I detest, I abhor their philosophy, but I detest more than that their tactics, which are those of the fifth column, and are dishonest. But at the same time I never as a citizen want to see our country become urged, by either fear or resentment of this group, that we ever compromise with any of our demo-cratic principles through that fear or resentment. I still think that democracy can do it.

Goldwater Speech: "A Time for Choosing"

OCTOBER 27, 1964

In October 1964, Reagan delivered a televised fund-raising speech for Republican presidential candidate Barry Goldwater. The senator and his campaign organization at first opposed the airing of the speech. Perhaps they feared that Reagan would overshadow Goldwater. They were right.

The speech, given only a week before the election, wouldn't stop the landslide of Goldwater's inevitable defeat, but it would help Reagan displace Goldwater as the star of conservative America. Reagan drafted the address himself, using the lines he had honed and polished in speeches across the country to local Rotary Clubs and chambers of commerce, where he would appear as the host of a television show called *GE Theater*.

In the Goldwater speech, Reagan again stressed the theme he had sounded across the nation:

And this idea that government is beholden to the people, that it has no other source of power except the sovereign people, is still the newest and the most unique idea in all the long history of man's relation to man.

This is the issue of this election: whether we believe in our capacity for self-government or whether we abandon the American Revolution and confess that a little intellectual elite in a far-distant capital can plan our lives for us better than we can plan them ourselves.

Reagan closed with lines from FDR and Lincoln:

You and I have a rendezvous with destiny. We'll preserve for our children this, the last best hope of man on earth, or we'll sentence them to take the last step into a thousand years of darkness.

Reagan's Concession Speech in Kansas City
AUGUST 19, 1976

In 1976 Reagan was running against an incumbent Republican president, Gerald Ford, who narrowly defeated him in the New Hampshire primary. From there it was downhill until the campaign moved to the South. In Florida and South Carolina, Reagan made Ford's negotiations to cede the Panama Canal the issue and Henry Kissinger its embodiment. He almost closed the gap in the hunt for delegates, but Ford still had a bare majority. John Sears, Reagan's campaign manager, dropped a bombshell by selecting moderate senator Dick Schweiker from Pennsylvania to be his running mate. It shook up the convention enough to breathe life into the Reagan cause, but it was not enough. He was counted out at 12:30 AM on August 19, when West Virginia's delegates, the last to be called, cast their votes for Ford.

A weary Reagan addressed his followers:

Don't get cynical, don't get cynical, because look at yourselves and what you were willing to do and recognize that there are millions and millions of Americans out there that want what you want, that want it to be that way, that want it to be a shining city on the hill.

His use of his favorite line came from Massachusetts governor John Winthrop's 1630 sermon; Winthrop had taken it from the Bible. In 1976, it brought tears to his supporters and his wife beside him. Reagan closed with an English ballad he had learned in childhood, letting those who believed in him know that they had not seen the last of Ronald Reagan.

> I'll lay me down and bleed a while
> Though I am wounded, I am not slain
> I shall rise and fight again.

Reagan's First Inaugural Address

JANUARY 20, 1981

On January 20, 1981, Ronald Reagan and his wife left Blair House in a limousine to cross the street to the White House to meet the Carters. President Carter and President-elect Reagan drove in one limousine to the Capitol, and their wives rode in another car. There was little conversation between the two men. Carter reportedly did not look Reagan in the eyes.

For his inaugural address, Reagan had told speechwriter Tony Dolan to strike three themes: first, his Jeffersonian principles of less government; second, as his hero FDR had addressed in his first inaugural, faith in the spirit of the American people to overcome adversity; and third, how the very nature of America produces heroes. Reagan then revised Dolan's draft.

For his political philosophy, he began with an aphorism he had used repeatedly on the speech circuit:

In this present crisis, government is not the solution to our problem; government is the problem. From time to time we've been tempted to believe that society has become too complex to be managed by self-rule, that government by an elite group is superior to government for, by, and of the people.

Later Reagan affirmed his faith in the greatness of the American people and the greatness of America's future—his answer to Carter's "malaise."

It is time for us to realize that we're too great a nation to limit ourselves to small dreams. We're not, as some would have us believe, doomed to an inevitable decline. I do not believe in a fate that will fall on us no matter what we do. I do believe in a fate that will fall on us if we do nothing. So with all the creative energy of our command, let us begin an era of national renewal. Let us renew our determination, our courage, and our strength. And let us renew our faith and hope.

He followed with a tribute to unsung American heroes:

We have every right to dream heroic dreams. Those who say that we are in a time when there are no heroes just don't know where to look. You can see heroes every day going in and out of factory gates. Others, a handful in number, produce enough food to feed all of us and then the world beyond. You meet heroes across a counter—and they are on both sides of that counter. There are entrepreneurs with faith in themselves and faith in an idea who create new jobs, new wealth, and opportunity. They are individuals and families whose taxes support the government and whose voluntary gifts support church, charity, culture, art, and education. Their patriotism is quiet but deep.

Reagan closed with what would become a patented ending to his major state addresses. It was a story of an unsung hero:

> Under one such [grave] marker [in Arlington Cemetery] lies a young man, Martin Treptow, who left his job in a small-town barbershop in 1917 to go to France with the famous Rainbow Division. There on the western front he was killed trying to carry a message between battalions under heavy artillery fire.
>
> We're told that on his body was found a diary. On the flyleaf under the heading "My Pledge" he had written these words: "America must win this war. Therefore, I will work, I will save, I will sacrifice, I will endure, I will fight cheerfully and do my utmost, as if the issue of the whole struggle depended on me alone."

The Palace of Westminster

JUNE 8, 1982

President Reagan traveled to London in June 1982 to deliver an address. He would be the first head of state to speak in the Palace of Westminster. Prime Minister Margaret Thatcher had invited him in reciprocation for her visit to Washington the previous February.

Tony Dolan, one of Reagan's principal speechwriters, saw in the remarks a history-making parallel to Churchill's Iron Curtain Address in 1946—a leader of the free world addressing a fellow English-speaking democracy at the invitation of the head of government. He saw it as a crusade for freedom. After thirty-six years, it was time to turn from the military defensive to the psychological offensive.

In writing the draft, Dolan looked to the Iron Curtain speech as his text. David Gergen, the head of the communications shop, thought the hard-right Dolan was the wrong choice for an European audience, whose perception of Reagan was as a kind of John Wayne—an actor/cowboy thought to be a little fast on the draw. But Dolan, anticipating such a reaction from Gergen, backchanneled it to Reagan. Reagan saw in it something he wanted to say as the leader of the free world.

Originally Reagan was to speak in Westminster Hall, but the objections of the Labour Party had forced a switch to the Great Gallery, which was just off the House of Lords. At seven o'clock, Reagan was ushered from the Robing Room into the Gallery. There, attended by the Beefeater Guards behind him and flanked by the Lord Chancellor on his right and the Speaker of the House on his left, Reagan began his address:

> Speaking for all Americans, I want to say how very much we feel at home in your house. Every American would, because this...is one of democracy's shrines.

Reagan then came right to his theme by citing British statesman William Gladstone on the developing solidarity movement in Poland. Gladstone, defending the Reform Bill in 1866, declared, "You cannot fight against the future. Time is on our side." Reagan added, "Optimism is in order because, day by day, democracy is proving itself to be a not at all fragile flower."

The next line was a deliberate attempt to echo Churchill's Iron Curtain words: "From Stettin on the Baltic to Varna on the Black Sea, the regimes planted by totalitarianism have had more than thirty years to establish their legitimacy. But none—not one regime—has yet been able to risk free elections."

Reagan then summarized with an aphorism, "Regimes planted by bayonets do not take root."

This maxim was reinforced by an underground Polish joke he had heard: "It is said that the Soviet Union would remain a one-party nation even if an opposition party were permitted, because everyone would join the opposition party."

Just as the chuckles of the audience were quieting, Reagan recharged the laughter by unleashing a Churchill *bon mot* about John Foster Dulles. Winston Churchill said (in exasperation) of one of America's most distinguished diplomats, "He is the only case I know of a bull who carries his china shop with him."

Reagan's audience roared with delight. The trademark self-deprecating humor won hearts even on the Labour side, among those who regarded Reagan's right-wing philosophy as even more unpalatable than Thatcher's. They found themselves beginning to like the genial Reagan, even if they might not like his views.

Reagan then turned somber as he discussed the Soviets' invasion of Afghanistan, their suppression of solidarity in Poland, and their use of toxic warfare. His reaction to Soviet aggression and brutality bore a stately cadence that could have been Churchill's: "If history teaches us anything, it teaches self-delusion in the face of unpleasant facts is folly." He then asked: "What, then, is our course? Must civilization perish in a hail of fiery atoms? Must freedom wither in a quiet, deadening accommodation with totalitarian evil?"

For his answer, Reagan quoted directly from Churchill's Iron Curtain Address: "I do not believe that Soviet Russia desires war. What they desire is the fruits of war and the indefinite expansion of their power and doctrines. But what we have to consider here today while time remains is the permanent prevention of war and the establishment of conditions of freedom and democracy as rapidly as possible in all countries."

The prophet of capitalism now turned to the prophet of communism to make his point:

> In an ironic sense Karl Marx was right. We are witnessing today a great revolutionary crisis, a crisis where the demands of the economic order are conflicting directly with those of the political order. But the crisis is happening not in the free, non-Marxist West, but in the home of Marxism-Leninism, the Soviet Union. It is the Soviet Union that runs against the tide of history by denying human freedom and human dignity to its citizens.

There are four institutions, Reagan went on to say, that define a free society and democracy: free press, unions, political parties, and universities.

Reagan then called for a prophetic plan: "What I am describing now is a plan and a hope for the long term—the march of freedom and democracy which will leave Marxism-Leninism on the ash heap of history."

He then returned to Churchill, quoting his address to the Joint Session of Congress in December 1941: "During the dark days of the Second World War, when this island was incandescent with courage, Winston Churchill exclaimed about Britain's adversaries, 'What kind of a people do they think we are?'"

He then rephrased the question: "So, let us ask ourselves, 'What kind of people do we think we are?' And let us answer, 'Free people, worthy of freedom and determined not only to remain so but to help others gain their freedom as well.'"

Reagan closed with this peroration, "Let us now begin a major effort to secure the best: a crusade for freedom that will engage the faith and fortitude of the next generation. For the sake of peace and justice, let us move toward a world in which all people are at last free to determine their own destiny.."

A former Conservative Party whip for Margaret Thatcher, John (now Lord) Cope, years later described the speech as "powerful, prophetic, and persuasive."

Lord Crathorne, who also heard it, said it was the greatest address he had ever heard. To a British audience that had too glibly accepted a caricature of the Hollywood President, Reagan had proved himself the leader of the free world. With the language of Churchill, he had turned the Marxist predictions upside down. He had delivered a prescription, as well as a prophesy, that did credit to the statesman he emulated.

"Evil Empire"

MARCH 8, 1983

On March 8, 1983, Reagan spoke to the National Association of Evangelicals—a convention of two thousand politically moderate Baptists and Methodists. The talk received little media hype beforehand, yet no two words he ever uttered would have more rhetorical impact.

Reagan outlined his theme just after the beginning paragraph of his remarks: "We know that living in this world means dealing with what philosophers would call the phenomenology of evil or, as theologians would put it, the doctrine of sin. There is sin and evil in the world, and we're enjoined by scripture and the Lord Jesus to oppose it with all our might."

He then referred to the recurring pressure of evil in our own history—such as slavery, racism, and anti-Semitism, all of which, he said, violated the precept "love they neighbor as thyself."

Reagan then turned to the Cold War, citing former Communist Whittaker Chambers: "Marxism-Leninism is actually the second-oldest faith, first proclaimed in the Garden of Eden with the words of temptation, 'Ye shall be as gods.'"

Speechwriter Tony Dolan had wanted Reagan to use the alliteration "evil empire" in his speech to the Houses of Parliament a year before, but the State

Department had considered those two words too inflammatory. Some also thought the reference to the movie *Star Wars* unpresidential. Showman Reagan, however, recognized that the catchy phrase, along with the pop culture connection, would resonate with the American people.

And so Reagan made a special appeal to these ministers who longed for peace, delivering the centerpiece of the speech: "So in your discussions of the nuclear freeze proposals I urge you to beware the temptation of pride—the temptation to blithely declare yourselves above it all and label both sides equally at fault, to ignore the facts of history and the aggressive impulses of an evil empire, to simply call the arms race a giant misunderstanding and thereby remove yourselves from the struggle between right and wrong and good and evil."

Pointe du Hoc, Normandy

JUNE 6, 1984

On the fortieth anniversary of D-Day, President Reagan delivered remarks at the U.S. Ranger Monument at Pointe du Hoc, France. It was more than a commemoration; it was a celebration of heroism and sacrifice. The Rangers had done the impossible task of scaling the almost vertical bluffs near the Normandy beach where the German guns fired down on the Allied landing troops.

The Ranger veterans were gathered before him, and he memorably praised them: "These are the boys of Pointe du Hoc. These are the men who took the cliffs. These are the champions who helped free a continent. These are the heroes who helped end a war."

Reagan recognized the Rangers' belief in themselves and their cause: "The men of Normandy had faith that what they were doing was right, faith that they fought for all humanity.... You were here to liberate, not to conquer, and so you and those others did not doubt your cause.... You all knew that some things are worth dying for. One's country is worth dying for, and democracy is worth dying for."

He then cited the Rangers' belief in God:

Something else helped the men of D-Day: their rock-hard belief that Providence would have a great hand in the events that would unfold here; that God was an ally in this great cause. And so, the night before the invasion, when Colonel Wolverton asked his parachute troops to kneel with him in prayer, he told them, "Do not bow your heads, but look up so you can see God and ask His blessing in what we're about to do." Also that night, General Matthew Ridgway on his cot, listening in the darkness for the promise God made to Joshua: "I will not fail thee nor forsake thee."

Here, in this place where the West held together, let us make a vow to our dead. Let us show them by our actions that we understand what they died for. Let our actions say to them the words for which Matthew Ridgway listened: "I will not fail thee nor forsake thee."

"Heal Humanity's Suffering"

MAY 9, 1985

In May 1985, President Reagan was scheduled for a European trip that included an economic summit in Bonn, West Germany. Chancellor Helmut Kohl had arranged a visit to a military cemetery in Bitburg. A press furor erupted when it was discovered that some Waffen-SS troops were buried there. Reagan resisted the demands to cancel the visit, and world attention was focused on the cemetery remarks. Reagan was cheered by a call to the White House by ninety-two-year-old General Matthew Ridgway, who offered to appear with the president at the event and suggested that a German general stand with them as well. They also planned a trip to the former concentration camp at Belsen. Former Nixon speechwriter Ken Khachigian was called in to work on a draft.

The final speech:

No one could visit there [Belsen] without deep and conflicting emotions. I felt great sadness that history could be filled with such waste, destruction, and evil, but my heart was also lifted by the knowledge that from the ashes has come hope and that from the terrors of the past we have built forty years of peace, freedom, and reconciliation among our nations. . . . We cannot undo the crimes and wars of yesterday nor call the millions back to life, but we can give meaning to the past by learning its lessons and making a better future. We can let our pain drive us to greater efforts to heal humanity's suffering.

The Challenger Disaster:
"We Will Never Forget Them"

JANUARY 28, 1986

On the morning before the president was scheduled to deliver the State of the Union address to Congress, the space shuttle *Challenger* exploded. Reagan called on speechwriter Peggy Noonan, whom he called his poet, to turn out a new speech by the evening. The address to the joint session of Congress was postponed by a week, and Reagan instead addressed the nation from the Oval Office.

Reagan opened by telling his television audience, "Today is a day for mourning and remembering. . . . We mourn seven heroes. . . . We mourn their loss as a nation together."

He then described the astronauts' unique qualities: "They had that special grace, that special spirit that says, 'Give me a challenge and I'll meet it with joy.' They had a hunger to explore the universe and discover its truths."

He then tried to explain how tragedies happen

And I want to say something to the schoolchildren of America who were watching the live coverage of the shuttle's takeoff. I know it is hard to understand, but sometimes painful things like this happen. It's all part of the process of exploration and discovery. It's all part of taking a chance and expanding man's horizons. The future doesn't belong to the fainthearted; it belongs to the brave.

Reagan reminded the audience that explorer Frances Drake had died in 1596 on that date aboard his ship: "In his lifetime the great frontiers were the oceans, and a historian later said, 'He lived by the sea, died on it, and was buried in it.' Well, today we can say of the *Challenger* crew: their dedication was, like Drake's, complete."

Reagan closed with a reference to "High Flight," a poem by John Gillespie Magee Jr., an American aviator who died in World War II: "We will never forget them, nor the last time we saw them, this morning as they prepared for their journey and waved goodbye and 'slipped the surly bonds of earth' to 'touch the face of God.'"

Moscow University

MAY 31, 1988

When President Reagan visited Moscow in 1988, he was struck with the contrast between the Kremlin Palace and the cold, drab structures of Communism. The people, he concluded, didn't have much; the wealth of the country was used to support the state.

Reagan did not know it at the time, but the Soviets allowed into the hall to hear the American president only those students who were members of the Young Communist League.

White House speechwriter Tony Dolan composed the draft, which was approved by the State Department. Reagan made only a few changes. He had told Dolan what he wanted his theme to be, and he came to that theme early in his talk:

Progress is not foreordained. The key is freedom—freedom of thought, freedom of information, freedom of communication. The renowned scientist, scholar, and founding father of this university, Mikhail Lomonosov, knew that. "It is common knowledge," he said, "that the achievements of science are considerable and rapid, particularly once the yoke of slavery is cast off and replaced by the freedom of philosophy."

Reagan told the students that freedom was surging in the world around them:

> Throughout the world, free markets are the model for growth. Democracy is the standard by which governments are measured....
>
> Freedom is the recognition that no single person, no single authority or government, has a monopoly on the truth; but that every individual life is infinitely precious, that every one of us put on this world has been put there for a reason and has something to offer.

Reagan then cited a litany of Soviet heroes to stress the search for truth: "Who, after all, needs to tell the land of Dostoevsky about the quest for truth, the home of Kandinski and Scriabin about imagination, the rich and noble culture of the Uzbek man of letters, Alisher Navoi, about beauty and heart?"

He added the words of Boris Pasternak from *Dr. Zhivago*: "What has for centuries raised man above the beast is not the cudgel, but an inward music—the irresistible power of unarmed truth."

Reagan closed his talk with a passage from Gogol's *Dead Souls*: "Comparing his nation to a speeding troika, Gogol asks what will be its destination. But he writes, 'There was no answer save the bell pouring forth marvelous sound.'"

Finally, he concluded:

In this Moscow spring, this May 1988, we may be allowed the hope that freedom, like the fresh green sapling planted over Tolstoy's grave, will blossom forth at last in the rich fertile soil of your people and culture. We may be allowed to hope that the marvelous sound of a new openness will keep rising through, ringing through, leading to a new world of reconciliation, friendship, and peace.

Farewell Address: "The Shining City"

January 11, 1989

George Washington first delivered a farewell presidential address and Dwight Eisenhower—another great general—revived it in January 1961.

In this speech, Reagan would feature his "supply side" economic philosophy which, to the dismay of his critics and most economists, had actually increased government revenues while cutting the people's taxes: "Common sense told us that when you put a big tax on something, the people will produce less of it. So we cut the people's tax rates, and the people produced more than ever before."

Reagan closed with that favorite image of his, that of Puritan governor John Winthrop's "city on a hill":

I've spoken of the shining city all my political life, but I don't know if I ever quite communicated what I saw when I said it. But in my mind it was a tall proud city built on rocks stronger than oceans, wind-swept, God-blessed, and teeming with people of all kinds living in harmony and peace, a city with free ports that hummed with commerce and creativity, and if there had to be city walls, the walls had doors and the doors were open to anyone with the will and the heart to get here. That's how I saw it and see it still.

Oxford Union: "Democracy's Next Battle"

DECEMBER 4, 1992

The Oxford Union is the oldest debating society in the world. It also prides itself as a prestigious forum for distinguished speakers. President Nixon chose it as his venue to return from California exile into public life in 1977. Through Oxford graduate and former prime minister Margaret Thatcher, the Society's student leaders secured a Reagan appearance, even though the faculty detested Reagan's politics almost as much as they did Thatcher's.

Reagan opened with a quotation from Oxford's most famous historian: "It was the British historian Arnold Toynbee who defined life as a voyage of discovery and not a safe harbor."

He then described his own voyage of life:

I have witnessed the birth of Communism and the death of Communism. I have seen the rise and fall of Nazi tyranny, the subsequent Cold War and the nuclear nightmare that for fifty years haunted the dreams of children everywhere. During that time my generation defeated totalitarianism, and more recently we have begun to destroy the weapons of mass destruction. As a result, your world is poised for better tomorrows.

Reagan then rhetorically asked the Oxford students. "What will you do on your journey?"

He answered: "As I see it, you have the opportunity to set and enforce international standards of civilized behavior. Does that sound unrealistic? It is not any larger a challenge than what my generation confronted."

Although the Oxford dons in attendance sat on their hands, the students rose in a roar of applause.

Acknowledgments

I am grateful to Steve Schuck. I am the Schuck Fellow for the Study of State-craft at the University of Colorado–Colorado Springs. This is a worthy title that is a fitting advance after being a Benjamin Franklin Fellow at the University of Pennsylvania (the Fels Institute of Government) and Woodrow Wilson Fellow at the International Center for Scholars at the Smithsonian. I also appreciate the assistance Schuck Foundation president Don Griffin has given me the past year.

I also thank Mary Jo and Jarvis Ryals for their previous support of me as Ryals Professor of Language and Leadership at Colorado State University in Pueblo. My continuing scholarship and authority of books would not be possible without such support.

Over the years, I have come to know many who were early members in the "Reagan Movement": *Reader's Digest's* executive editor Bill Schulz, Ambassador Faith Whittelsey, White House staffer Anne Higgins, mail advertising wizard Richard Viguerie, and conservative polemicist Pat Buchanan. Chris Ruddy, editor in chief of NewsMax.com, is an old friend and Reagan apostle.

I always count too on the advice of my close friend and associate John LeBoutillier, who served in Congress during Reagan's first term.

In the mechanical preparation for this book, I want to thank Lia Sissom of Colorado State University in Pueblo, whose enthusiasm for Reagan is attested to by her son Johnathan Reagan Sissom.

I am particularly grateful to the advice and assistance of Kyle Dorrell in the preparation of this manuscript.

Linda Graham has also assisted in typing, and Regnery Publishing's Tim Carney in editing. And I thank the tireless Will Sherlin of the Carol Mann Agency, my literary agency.

Index

A

abortion, 4
acting, 4, 95
Adams, John, 105
affirmative action, 4
Afghanistan, 191
age, 5, 35, 45, 105, 126, 146
Alexander, Grover Cleveland, 117
Alzheimer's month, 89
America, 5–6, 184, 205
Americans, 6–7, 187
Anderson, John, 125, 129
Anderson, Martin, 77
appeasement, 8
arms treaties, 8, 123
Army relief, 116
"ash heap of history" speech,
    189–93
assassination attempt, 110, 124,
    128, 129, 166, 167

Astaire, Fred, 113
astrology, 102
atheism, 36
autobiography, 130

B

Baker, Howard, 125
Baker, James A., 71, 72, 76
balanced budget, 37
Baldrige, Mac, 57
Bedtime for Bonzo, 90, 157
Belsen concentration camp, 198
Bergman, Ingrid, 108
Berlin, Irving, 116
Berlin Wall, 8, 127–128
Bible, 106
big government, 9
bigotry, 9, 104

Bitburg military cemetery, 198
blueberry jelly beans, 99
Bond, Ward, 160
Boru, Brian, 114
Brandenberg Gate, 127–128
Brezhnev, Leonid, 41, 137
Brother Rat, 104
Brown, Edmund "Pat," 71, 77,
  102
Brown, Willie, 164
Bryan, William Jennings, 179
budget deficits, 38, 165
bureaucrats and bureaucracy, 37,
  135, 138, 149
Burke's Peerage, 114
Bush, George H. W., 55, 72, 103,
  120, 125, 126
Bush, George W., 120, 178

C
Cagney, James, 107, 111, 130
California, 37

California governorship, 42, 102,
  148, 163
Cannon, Lou, 72
capitalism, 10, 19, 137
Carter, Jimmy, 54, 56, 121, 129, 186
Casablanca, 108
Cassavetes, John, 101
Challenger space shuttle, 100, 200–1
Chambers, Whittaker, 194
Chesterfield cigarettes, 116
Chicago Cubs, 113, 146
China, 56
Christianity, xi, 21, 59, 106. *See also*
  religious faith
Churchill, Winston, 57, 129, 189,
  191, 192
citizenship, 10, 15
civil decline, 15
civil liberties, 11
Cleveland, Grover, 92
Clifford, Clark, 73
Clinton, Bill, 120
Coburn, Charles, 130

Cohan, George M., 111
Cold War, 11, 70, 81, 165, 194
collectivism, 159
Communism, 12, 13, 76, 111, 150, 180, 190
concession speech, 184–185
Congress, 25, 38
conservatism, 13, 58
Constitution of the United States, 14, 25, 38
Cooper, Gary, 100
Cooper, Rocky, 100
Cope, John, 193
courage, 14
Crathorne, Lord, 193
"The Cremation of Sam McGee" (Service), 162
crime, 14
Cummings, Robert, 70, 109

D
D-Day, 15, 196–97

Davis, Patti, 73
Day, Doris, 113, 117
de Havilland, Olivia, 70, 160, 180
de Valera, Éamon, 98
Dead Souls (Gogol), 203
Deaver, Michael, 71, 74, 142, 144, 171
debates, 125, 126, 129
defense, 15
democracy, 13, 15, 16, 181, 190, 192, 203
Democrats, 16, 140, 157
Dempsey, Jack, 124
depression, economic, 39, 56
divorce, 95
Dixon, Illinois, x, 96, 112, 151, 169
Dixon, Jeanne, 102
Doctor Zhivago (Pasternak), 203
doctorate, 39
Dolan, Tony, 74, 179, 186, 189, 194, 202
Dole, Bob, 125
Donaldson, Sam, 157

Drake, Francis, 201
D'Souza, Dinesh, 75
Dukakis, Michael, 54, 58
Dulles, John Foster, 191
duty, 144

E
Eastwood, Clint, 157
economic recovery, 56
economists, 39, 136, 175
economy: conservatism and, 13;
    depression vs. recession, 39, 56;
    foreign trade, 30; free markets
    and, 19; poverty and, 24;
    Reaganomics and, 16
education, 40, 47
Edwards, Jim, 170
Eisenhower, Dwight D., 120, 149,
    164, 205
El Alamein, 101
Elizabeth, Queen Mother, 162
Elizabeth II, 114, 150, 162

environment, 170
"evil empire" speech, 194–95
eyesight, 89, 98

F
facts, 17
faith. *See* religious faith
family, 18
farewell address, ix, 205
fate, 18
Federal Election Commission, 125
First Amendment, 11
first inaugural address, 186
Flynn, Errol, 145, 160, 165
football, 40, 90, 117
Ford, Gerald, 75, 103, 105, 117,
    120, 144, 151, 173, 184
foreign policy, 18, 41, 173
free market, 19, 137
free society, 192
freedom, 19, 193; American, 5–6;
    Communism and, 13; foreign

policy and, 18; as key to progress, 202

Frisch, Frankie, 158

future, 20

G

Gas House Gang, 158

General Electric, 2, 140, 174

George Washington University, 39

George Washington University Hospital, 128, 166

Gergen, David, 189

Gerson, Michael, 178

Gilder, Josh, 179

Gipp, George, 90, 131

Gladstone, William, 190

God, 21

Gogol, Nikolai, 203

Goldwater, Barry, 58, 70, 182

Gorbachev, Mikhail, 74, 122, 123, 127, 137, 153, 165, 172

government, 9, 31, 37, 41, 42, 182, 186

governorship, 42, 102, 148, 163

Graham, Billy, 109

Great Communicator, ix, 2, 97, 178

Great Society, 23, 42

H

Haig, Alexander, Jr., 41, 75, 134

Hannaford, Peter, 128

Harriman, Averell, 38

Harrison, William Henry, 105

Hart, Gary, 35

The Hasty Heart, 98, 106, 145

Hayden, Sterling, 76

health, 43, 94

hearing, 43

Heflin, Van, 160

Hellcats of the Navy, 92

Henreid, Paul, 109

heroes, 21, 54, 187
"High Flight" (Magee), 100, 201
Hinckley, John, 124
history, 20, 44, 60
Holden, William, 97, 113
Hollywood, 22, 76
Hollywood Independent Citizens' Committee of the Arts, Sciences, and Professions, 180
Hoover, Herbert, 82
Hope, Bob, 168
Hopper, Hedda, 96
horses, 101
House Un-American Activities Committee, 180
Humes, James C., 173

I

Iceland, 123
inaugural address, 186
Iran-Contra affair, 143
Iron Curtain speech, 189, 192

J

James, Daniel "Chappie," 59
James, Henry, 80
Jefferson, Thomas, 36
jelly beans, 99
Jelly Belly, 99
Jesus Christ, 59
John Paul II, 30
Johnny Belinda, 93
Johnson, Andrew, 92
Jurges, Billy, 146

K

Kemp, Jack, 125
Kennedy, Edward, 38, 78
Kennedy, John F., 26, 60, 120, 178
KGB, 43
Khachigian, Ken, 198
The Killers, 101
King, Martin Luther, Jr., 55
Kings Row, 109, 111, 130
Kirkpatrick, Jeane, 77
Kissinger, Henry, 61, 73, 103, 184

Knights of the Round Table, 115
Knute Rockne: All American, 90, 131
Kohl, Helmut, 198

L

law and order, 44
Laxalt, Paul, 103
Leslie, Joan, 116
Lewis, Anthony, 78
liberalism, 44, 175
lifeguard duty, 112
Lincoln, Abraham, x–xi, 67, 72,
    134, 149, 183
Little Red Hen parable, 154
Lomonosov, Mikhail, 202
looks, 45
Lucky, 142

M

MacFarlane, Robert, 79
Magee, John Gillespie, Jr., 100, 201
malaise, 187

marijuana, 22
marriage, 22, 92, 97
Marvin, Lee, 101
Marx, Karl, 60, 192
Massey, Raymond, 160
Massie, Robert, 79
Meese, Edwin, 76
middle age, 45
military service, 116
Mitterrand, François, 80
Mondale, Walter, 54, 61, 126, 146
Moretti, Bob, 81
Moscow University speech, 135,
    202–204
Moses, 35, 38
Mother Teresa, 66, 84
Murphy, George, 102, 180

N

National Anthem, 23
National Association of Evangeli-
    cals, 194
national debt, 45

Neal, Patricia, 145
New Deal, 23
New Hampshire primary, 125
nicknames, 82, 90, 113, 131
Nixon, Richard M., 28, 34, 56, 173, 178, 206
Noonan, Peggy, 80, 83, 179, 200
Normandy. *See* D-Day
Notre Dame, 131
Nunn, Sam, 62

O

O'Brien, Pat, 90, 131
O'Neill, Tip, 45, 54, 62, 82, 134, 166
Osborne, John, 82
Oxford Union speech, 206–207

P

Panama Canal, 23, 184
parables, 154

Parr, Jerry, 124
Parsons, Luella, 96
Pasternak, Boris, 203
Peanuts comic strip, 142
Pointe du Hoc, 54, 196–197
poise, 46
Poland, 30, 152, 190
politics, 46
Portillo, José López, 101
Portugal, 150
poverty, 24, 47
Power, Tyrone, 100
pragmatism, 24
prayer, 25
presidency, 26, 47
presidential debates, 125, 126, 129
Price, Ray, 178
progress, 202

Q

Qadhafi, Muammar, 62

R

Radio Free Europe, 152
radio host, 97, 113, 117, 146–47, 178
Raft, George, 109
Reagan, Jack, 82, 104, 169
Reagan, Maureen, 95, 108
Reagan, Michael, x, 95, 108, 141, 167
Reagan, Nancy, 63, 83, 92, 97, 110, 168, 171
Reagan, Nell Wilson, 63
Reagan, Ronald, on himself, 21, 43, 47, 206
Reaganomics, 16, 136
recession, 39, 56
Regan, Donald, 63
religious faith, xi, 17, 21, 25, 36, 59, 63, 106, 197
religious oppression, 27
Reykjavik summit, 122–123
Ridgway, Matthew, 197, 198
Rockne, Knute, 90, 131

Rogers, Roy, 113
Rogers, Will, 16
Roosevelt, Franklin D., 23, 26, 55, 92, 111, 179, 180, 183
Roosevelt, Jimmy, 180
Roosevelt, Theodore, 7, 26, 64

S

Sadat, Anwar, 65
Saint Peter, 161
Santa Fe Trail, 145, 160
school, 47
Schroeder, Pat, 81
Schultz, Charles, 142
Schweiker, Dick, 139, 184
Screen Actors Guild, 93, 111, 180
screen test, 107
Sears, John, 125, 184
Secret Service code names, 110
self-government, 182, 186
Service, Robert, 162
shining city, 184, 205

Shultz, George, 123
Sinatra, Frank, 54, 109
smoking, 27, 116
Snoopy for president, 142
social programs, 31
socialism, 154, 159, 169
Solidarity movement, 190
Sorenson, Ted, 178
Soviet Union: on ash heap of history, 189–93; Berlin Wall and, 127–28; capitalism and, 10; collectivism, 159; Communism and, 12–13; as evil empire, 28, 194–95; foreign policy and, 41; invasion of Afghanistan, 191; Moscow University speech, 202–4; nuclear weapons and, 122–23; as one-party system, 48; political freedom in, 153
space shuttle disaster, 100, 200–1
Speakes, Larry, 36
special interests, 28
speech writing, 74, 178–79

sportscasting, 113, 117, 146
St. John's Episcopal Church (Washington), 100
St. Louis Cardinals, 158
stage names, 113
Stahl, Lesley, 84
Star Wars, 123, 195
statesmanship, 29
status quo, 48
Stewart, Jimmy, 54, 61
Stockman, David, 129
Strategic Defense Initiative (SDI), 123, 165
student protests, 122, 148
supply side economics, 205
Supreme Court, 25

T

tax cuts, 29, 141, 165
taxation, 49
taxes: big government and, 9; conservatism and, 13; Democrats

and, 16; parable on, 154–55;
   welfare state and, 31
taxpayer, 50
Taylor, Robert, 54, 64, 180
Temple, Shirley, 94, 114
Ten Commandments, 38
terrorism, 29
That Hagen Girl, 94, 114
Thatcher, Margaret, 54, 65, 81,
   129, 189, 206
Third World, 173
This Is the Army, 116
Thomas, J. Parnell, 180
"A Time for Choosing," 179, 182
Todd, Richard, 106, 145
totalitarianism, 190
Toynbee, Arnold, 206
trade, 30
tragedy, 200
Treptow, Martin, 188
Truman, Harry S., 26, 34
Tunney, Gene, 124
tyranny, 30

U

University of California, 148
unsung heroes, 187–88
U.S. Ranger monument, 196

V

vice president selection, 102
Vietnam War protests, 148
Viguerie, Richard, 65
Von Hoffman, Nicholas, 85

W

Warner, Jack, 84, 109
Warner Brothers, 107, 111, 130
Washington, D.C., 50
Washington, George, 66, 67, 205
Washington Post, 164
Wayne, John, 54, 189
wedding, 97
Weicker, Lowell, 60
Weinberger, Caspar W., 64

welfare state, 31, 51
Will, George, 83, 85
The Winning Team, 117
Winthrop, John, 185, 205
Wolverton, Robert L., 197
work, 51
World Affairs Council of Philadel-
  phia, 173

Wyman, Jane, 93, 95, 96, 104, 108,
  113

Y

Yankee Doodle Dandy, 111, 130
Young Communist League, 202
Young Presidents' Organization, 151